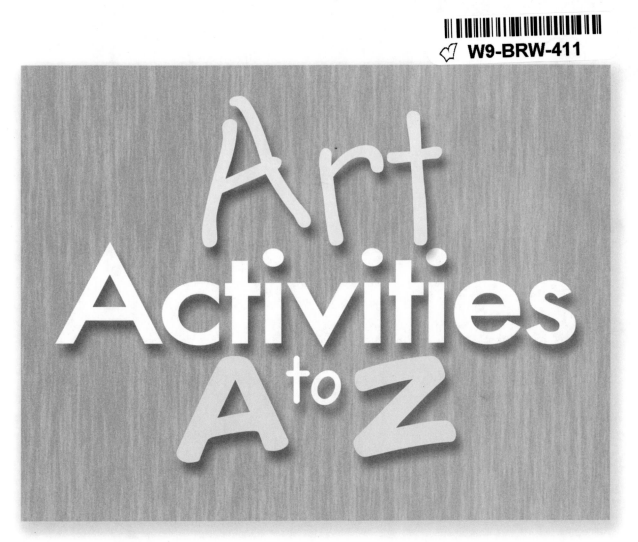

Join us on the web at
EarlyChildEd.delmar.com

Joanne Matricardi
Jeanne McLarty

THOMSON

DELMAR LEARNING

Australia Canada Mexico Singapore Spain United Kingdom United States

THOMSON

DELMAR LEARNING

Art Activities A to Z
Joanne Matricardi and Jeanne McLarty

Vice President, Career Education SBU:
Dawn Gerrain

Director of Editorial:
Sherry Gomoll

Acquisitions Editor:
Erin O'Connor

Editorial Assistant:
Stephanie Kelly

Director of Production:
Wendy A. Troeger

Production Editor:
Joy Kocsis

Production Assistant:
Angela Iula

Director of Marketing:
Wendy E. Mapstone

Cover Design:
Joseph Villanova

Composition:
Pre-Press Company, Inc.

Printed in Canada
1 2 3 4 5 XXX 08 07 06 05

For more information contact Thomson Delmar Learning, Executive Woods, 5 Maxwell Drive, Clifton Park, NY 12065-2919.

Or find us on the World Wide Web at www.thomsonlearning.com, www.delmarlearning.com, or www.earlychilded.delmar.com

Library of Congress Cataloging-in-Publication Data

Matricardi, Joanne.
  Art activities A to Z / Joanne Matricardi and Jeanne McLarty.
    p. cm. — (Activities A to Z series)
  Includes bibliographical references and index.
  ISBN 1-4018-7164-X (alk. paper)
 1. Art—Study and teaching (Early childhood) 2. Early childhood education—Activity programs. 3. English language—Alphabet—Study and teaching (Early childhood) I. McLarty, Jeanne. II. Title.
  LB1139.5.A78M38 2005
  372.5—dc22

2004023852

NOTICE TO THE READER

Contents

Preface

Art is an important part of a quality preschool program, integrating all areas of the curriculum. In order to be effective, art must be creative, open-ended, and process-centered. The preschooler enjoys art for the joy of movement and the sensory experience.

If done correctly, preschool art enhances all areas of development. It promotes intellectual development through the use of many mediums. It allows children to make decisions about what to use. Art develops creative thought as the child selects supplies. Art also encourages social development, teaching children to share materials and helping them develop responsibility in taking care of those materials. Preschool art also allows for emotional expression; the messy activities can help the child release stress and tensions. Finally, art promotes physical development. Large and small muscles are exercised as the child is allowed freedom of movement in the execution of strokes and the management of various tools.

This resource book is designed for preschool teachers, parents of young children, and early childhood students. Teachers need to be awakened to the various potentials of the art process. *Art Activities A to Z* moves them through a world of possibilities beyond paint and brushes. It is also formatted to help those teachers who want to incorporate a letter of the week into their curriculum.

Art Activities A to Z is helpful to parents who want to encourage their children's creativity. Many of the activities focus on supplies found in the kitchen and at home. The open-ended art activities, done at home, will be beneficial to the child and family as they create together. Art can become a transition between home and school.

This book also benefits early childhood students, because most have difficulty moving away from product-centered crafts. *Art Activities A to Z* is the introduction and tool needed to stimulate creativity. A lesson plan format is used to further aid those who are new to the teaching profession.

Each section of this book will assist teachers and parents in finding art projects for a theme-based curriculum, for letter-of-the-week activities, or as spur-of-the-moment fillers. Detailed instruction is given in a lesson plan format for each of the activities. Age appropriateness is suggested. When looking at the recommended age range for the activities, please consider the abilities of your children, and your staff ratio. The ages suggested are given in consideration of the materials, attention span, and ability of the children to do the activity by themselves. You as a teacher or parent know your children best. Although age appropriateness is recommended, the teacher, parent, or student should feel free to experiment out of the age ranges listed.

The lesson plans provided include five sections: "Developmental Goals," "Learning Objective," "Materials," "Adult Preparation," and "Procedures." "Developmental Goals" describe the benefits the child derives from the art process. The "Learning Objective" states the behavioral outcome of the activity and what tools the children will use to achieve that outcome. In most cases, the behavioral objective is simply for the child to experience a new art form. The "Materials" section allows the teacher or parent to gather all supplies needed for the activity. "Adult Preparation" details the work to be done before the child becomes involved in the process. However, older children are welcome to share this experience. "Procedures" are a step-by-step recipe for the child to successfully engage in the activity. Additional sections for some activities include "Variations," "Expansions," or "Activity Suggestions." These provide for the use of different techniques or show ways to allow the experience to be molded to specific preschool themes. A "Safety Precaution" is included with some of the activities. Sometimes, this is to alert the teacher or parent of very young children that the materials used are small items that present a choking hazard, so choking precautions are indicated. Other activities involve the use of heat, and an appropriate "Safety Precaution" is listed for each of these experiences. Please perform these activities with close supervision.

Art Activities A to Z includes food items as another art medium. A center may choose not to paint with food, depending on its policies. Please use at your own discretion. Substitutions have been added when available.

This book concludes with a theme-specific index. Teachers may reference this list to complement traditional units that are used with young children. For example, "Acorn Painting" is indexed under "Fall." Of course, many of these activities can be used for themes other than those under which they are indexed. "Acorn Painting" could also be part of a gardening unit, because items such as beans and baby carrots are listed as alternative materials.

Art is intended to be a joyful, creative experience. Use the activities that you enjoy most; your enthusiasm will be contagious!

ANCILLARY MATERIAL

ONLINE COMPANION™

The Online Companion™ is an accompaniment to *Art Activities A to Z*. This site contains additional hands-on art activities for young children. The activities are written in the same lesson plan format found in this book. These detailed plans include developmental goals, learning objectives, a list of materials, directions for adult preparation, and a step-by-step procedure for the child. The activities are easy to understand and implement, either in the preschool classroom or at home. Creativity is the focus as young children engage in process-oriented activities.

The *Art Activities A to Z* Online Companion™ also provides links to related preschool sites. These links contain art ideas, supplies, and materials. Please visit www.earlychilded.delmar.com to gain access to this Online Companion™.

ACKNOWLEDGMENTS

This book is an accumulation of original and shared ideas developed over 40 years of teaching young children. Many thanks to our co-workers, students, and their parents for sharing and experimenting with us.

We would like to express our appreciation of Terry McLarty and Josh McLarty, our technical advisors. Thanks also go to Kathy Gosman, Julie Fowkes, Robin Pestorius, and Vicki Ziegler for critiquing and sharing our ideas with their classes.

We, and the editors at Thomson Delmar Learning, would also like to thank the following reviewers for their time, effort, and thoughtful contributions which helped to shape the final text:

Wendy Bertoli, M. Ed.
Lancaster County Career and
Technology Center
Mount Jay, PA

Patricia Capistron
Rocking Unicorn Preschool
West Chatham, MA

Heather Fay
Child care Consultant
Akron, OH

Vicki Folds, Ed.D.
Broward Community College
Coconut Creek, FL

Jody Martin
Crème de la Crème
Golden, CO

Judy Rose-Paterson
Childtime Children's Centers
Escondido, CA

Joanne Matricardi
Jeanne McLarty

HELPFUL HINTS

Through years of experience, we've developed techniques that help our activities go more smoothly. Some are simple tricks to make cleanup easier. Others are strategies to ensure the success of activities. The following helpful hints have become routine in our classrooms.

✄ **Mix tempera paint with liquid dish soap,** which makes it easier to wash paint out of clothes and off of hands. Use approximately one tablespoon of dish soap to one cup of tempera paint.

✄ **Insert plastic sandwich bags into paint containers** to make cleanup easier. (You may purchase paint containers or use empty frosting containers.) Put a plastic bag into the container, then put paint and dish soap into the baggie. A lid may be put on the container if it is to be used for more than one day. When you are through with the paint, simply throw the bag away, leaving a clean container.

✄ **Use empty plastic snack-size applesauce and fruit containers for paint or glue** when the full-size cups are not needed.

✄ **Use foam trays, plates, or plastic lids** when a limited amount of paint is needed. Using plastic or foam plates may encourage recycling, because they can be cleaned and reused. The foam plate or plastic lid is a necessity for use with liquid watercolor. Foam and plastic repel the watercolor, whereas paper will absorb it, requiring the use of more watercolor and extra cleanup.

✄ **Make a paint blotter** by pouring a limited amount of tempera paint into a foam tray or plate. Mix the paint with dish soap and then lay a folded paper towel on top of the paint. The paper towels should be folded according to the size of the tray or plate. Use one or two paper towels, depending on the thickness of the towels. Then flip the towel over, revealing the paint. Using this method limits the amount of paint required and prevents blobs from forming on the child's paper. The towel may be flipped as needed, keeping the paint fresh and available in the necessary proportion.

✄ **Make stamp pads from foam shoe inserts** (found in the foot-care section of groceries, pharmacies, and discount stores). One package (two foam inserts) makes four stamp pads. Cut each insert in half. Dampen the insert with water. Lay on a small tray or foam plate. Add liquid watercolor or food coloring, and the stamp pad is ready. Shoe inserts are especially good to use when making food prints. Rinse the inserts when finished, and let them air dry.

✂ **Cut fruits or vegetables for print making in advance and allow sufficient time for them to dry,** thus ensuring that paints or watercolors will adhere to them. Fruits cut and used immediately will retain their natural juices and will be difficult to paint with. A general rule is to cut and air-dry citrus fruit the night before use. Cut items such as apples and potatoes 20–30 minutes before they are used.

✂ **Make handles on fruits or vegetables used in making prints** by putting a metal fork or a corncob holder into the top of the food. This helps younger children or those with special needs to be successful holding the fruit or vegetable.

✂ **Color pasta, rice, or eggshells** by putting them into a resealable plastic bag or a jar with a lid and adding food coloring or liquid watercolor and a capful of rubbing alcohol. Shake the bag or jar until all the items are colored. Pour onto newsprint or paper towels to dry.

✂ **Use stained grits, salt, or sand instead of glitter** if your center's policies prevent glitter use. Color grits with liquid watercolor. (Do not add rubbing alcohol, which would make the grits gummy.) Add dry tempera paint to salt or sand.

✂ **Use liquid watercolors in place of food coloring** to eliminate mixing to achieve different hues. Liquid watercolors, which are brilliant and washable, may be ordered through a school supply catalog.

✂ **Vary paintbrush sizes according to the age of the child or activity.** For younger children, use wider brushes. This enables them to get more paint onto the paper, thus accommodating their short attention spans. For a variation, **use cotton swabs** for children ages two and older. This will greatly enhance their fine motor skills.

✂ **Use nontoxic school glue for safety and easy cleanup.** White school glue is preferred. The clear glue can't be mixed with other substances or diluted with water as easily.

✂ **Pour glue into milk bottle caps for use by younger children.** Each child may then spread the glue with a cotton swab or paintbrush (depending on age and fine motor skills). This limits the amount of glue put onto the paper.

✂ **Use diluted glue to cover a large area;** mix two parts glue with one part water. Children can spread the glue across a large area, using a wide brush.

✂ **Provide a bucket of warm soapy water and paper towels** for easy cleanup if there is no sink in your art center or classroom.

✂ **Use a tray or cookie sheet with finger paints,** which allows the child time to experiment and enjoy the sensory experience without tearing the paper from overuse. Once the child is finished, lay paper over the finger-painting activity and rub to make a print.

We're often asked, "How many children should be allowed to come to the art center at a time?" The answer may seem vague, but it depends on the age of the children, their temperament, and what the activity is. Typically, age is the dominant factor:

Age	Number of Children at the Art Center
Toddlers	1
2-year-olds	2
3- to 5-year-olds	3–5

The age rule should simply be a guide. Some activities require much more supervision than others. If the activity includes using hot surfaces, one-to-one supervision is required, no matter what the age is in your classroom. And then there are those years when the temperament of your classroom may require that you do most activities with a reduced ratio.

Art with toddlers requires different management skills. The teacher of one-year-olds is often called away from the art table to attend to children. As a safety and cleanliness measure, we have found that putting all of the toddler's art supplies on a tray alleviates most problems. For example, we set a tray containing paper, paint, and brush on the table in front of the child. When the child is finished and needs assistance with hand washing, the teacher simply sets the tray up out of reach until she is ready for the next child to begin the activity.

SUPPLIES NEEDED

Most early childhood programs operate on a limited budget. Thus, many of the materials we use in this book may be purchased at grocery, hardware, office/school supply, and discount stores. We provide a shopping list for your convenience. Also included is a sample family letter for use when requesting recycled and household items.

SHOPPING LIST

Adding machine tape
Aluminum foil
Baby wipes
Balloons
Baseballs
Bath towels
Bingo bottles
Birdseed
Bowls
Broom—child size
Bubble wrap
Bulletin board paper
Can opener
Chalk
Child-size oven mitt
Clothespins (spring)
Coffee filters
Coffee grounds
Colored pencils
Combs
Construction paper
Cookie sheets
Copy paper
Corn syrup (light)
Cotton balls
Cotton swabs
Craft sticks
Crayons
Dental floss
Disposable latex
    gloves
Disposable plastic
    gloves
Doilies
Doll hair
Dried beans
Drop cloth
Dry erase markers
Empty salt shakers
Eyedroppers
Feather dusters

Feathers
Feathers—large, with
    pronounced tip
Flyswatters
Fluorescent tempera
    paint
Food coloring
Foam insulation tape
    (self-adhesive)
Foam shoe inserts
Foam plates
Foam roller brushes
    (child-size)
Forks (various sizes)
Gel pens
Gelatin (flavored)
Glitter
Gold spray paint
Grease screens
Grits
Hand lotion
Ice cube tray
Jingle bells
Joy® dish soap
Knife (for adult use)
Lace (flat, wide)
Large plastic sheet
Liquid dish soap
Liquid starch
Liquid watercolors
Magnetic marbles
Magnetic wands
Markers (water based)
Marshmallows
Masking tape
Measuring cups
Measuring spoons
Mirror
Muffin tin
Netting
Newspaper roll
Newsprint

Nonmenthol shaving
    cream
Nylon bath puff
Nuts and bolts
Oatmeal
Oilcans (empty)
Paintbrushes (various
    sizes)
Pantyhose
Paper clips
Paper doilies
Paper grocery bags
Paper lunch bags
Paper plates
Paper towels
Petroleum jelly
Plaster of Paris
Plastic covering for
    floor
Plastic eggs
Plastic forks
Plastic jelly beans
Plastic pizza cutters
Plastic spoons
Plastic straws
Plastic trays
Plastic worms
Plastic wrap
Plungers
Poster board
Powdered drink mix
    (unsweetened)
Push pins
Resealable plastic
    bags
Resealable plastic
    freezer bags
Rice
Rick rack
Rope
Rubber bands (various
    sizes and lengths)

Rubbing alcohol
Ruler
Sand
Sandwich bags
School glue (white)
Scrapers
Scissors
Sequins
Serving trays
Shakers (empty
    containers)
Small dustpans
Small spray bottles
Small squirt bottles
Sponges
Sponge brushes
Squeeze containers
Stapler and staples
Stencils
Stickers
Sticks (assorted)
Strawberry baskets
Table salt
Tag board
Tempera paint (dry)
Tempera paint (liquid)
Tissue paper (various
    colors)
Toothbrushes
Tongue depressors
Toy horseshoes
Tubes of toothpaste
Vegetable oil
Washcloth
Watercolors (dry in
    trays)
Wax candles
Wax paper
Whisk brooms
Wooden blocks
Yo-yos

FAMILY LETTER

Dear Family,

Many of the items we use in our art center may be found at home. Please save the following circled items and have your child bring them to school.

2-liter soda bottles
20-ounce soda bottles with caps
35mm film canisters
Assorted plastic lids
Baby food jars with lids
Coffee cans
Cookie cutters
Cookie sheets
Electric skillet
Empty roll-on deodorant bottles
Empty snack-size fruit containers
Empty tin cans
Flowers (colorful)
Golf balls
Keys
Knee-high stockings
Lace
Milk caps
Mismatched gloves
Mismatched socks
Newspaper
X-rays
Pans—assorted sizes
Paint shirts/smocks
Paper towel rolls

Pie pans
Pint-size strawberry baskets
Plastic containers with lids
Plastic ice cream buckets
Potato mashers
Pump soap dispensers
Record player
Ribbons
Rinsed eggshells
Rolling pins
Salad spinners
Scraps of wood
Small shampoo bottles
Squeeze bottles
Spatulas
Foam egg cartons
Tennis balls
Thread spools (empty)
Toilet paper rolls (empty)
Toy xylophone with mallet
Twist ties
Wallpaper scraps
Wire colanders
Warming tray
Yarn

Thanks for your help!

Sincerely,

Absorption

ADULT PREPARATION:

1. Pour liquid watercolor into small containers. Use one container for each color.
2. Fold coffee filters into fourths.

PROCEDURES:

The child will complete the following steps:

1. Hold the folded tip of a coffee filter; dip the open ends into liquid watercolor, while counting 1, 2, 3.
2. Watch as the filter absorbs the color.
3. Lay the filter on a newspaper to dry.
4. Repeat steps 1–3 with other filters, using other colors.

ACTIVITY SUGGESTION:

When filters are dry, layer different-colored filters. Twist the different colored filters together from the center, then staple them onto a leaf cutout. This may be used for a Mother's Day corsage.

AGES: 2–5

DEVELOPMENTAL GOALS:

- ✂ To develop creativity
- ✂ To observe a transformation of colors by mixing them

LEARNING OBJECTIVE:

Using coffee filters and liquid coloring, the child will dip the filters into the coloring and watch as the filters absorb color.

MATERIALS:

Round coffee filters
Liquid watercolor or food coloring
Small containers
Newspaper

Acorn Painting

DEVELOPMENTAL GOALS:

- ✄ To enhance motor skills
- ✄ To delight in movement and rhythm

LEARNING OBJECTIVE:

Using a box, paint, paper, and acorns, the child will paint with a new medium.

MATERIALS:

Box (to fit the size of the paper)
Gallon ice cream bucket with lid (for younger children)
Pie pan (for older children)
Fall colors of tempera paint
Water
Paint containers
Spoons
Acorns
Construction paper

ADULT PREPARATION:

1. Cut the construction paper to fit the bucket, box, or pie pan.
2. Pour tempera paint into a paint container; mix with water (two parts paint to one part water).
3. Add two or three acorns to each container of paint.

PROCEDURES:

The child will complete the following steps:

1. Put paper into pan or bucket.
2. Drain excess paint from acorn with spoon and then spoon the acorn into the pan or bucket.
3. **Younger children:** With adult assistance, put the lid on the bucket, then shake the bucket. **Older children:** Gently move the pan from side to side, allowing the acorn to roll around the paper leaving a trail of paint.
4. Repeat steps 1–3, using other colors.

continued

Acorn Painting continued

SAFETY PRECAUTION:

For ages 1–2, the teacher will perform steps 1–2 of the procedures. Be sure to use a container with a lid for younger children, because acorns may present a choking hazard. For younger children, only the teacher handles the acorns. Supervision is required.

VARIATION:

Use dried beans, baby carrots, marbles, mixed nuts (still in the shell), or jelly beans instead of acorns.

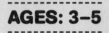
DEVELOPMENTAL GOALS:

- ✂ To develop eye-hand coordination
- ✂ To develop muscular coordination

LEARNING OBJECTIVE:

Using adding machine tape, cotton swabs, brushes, and watercolors, the child will create a design.

MATERIALS:

Adding machine tape
Watercolors (set of watercolors or liquid watercolors)
Containers for liquid watercolors
Brushes
Cotton swabs
Stapler
Plastic straws—one for each child
Rubber bands—one for each child

Adding Machine Tape Art

ADULT PREPARATION:

1. Cut a section of adding machine tape for each child, approximately 2–3 feet long.

PROCEDURES:

1. The child will create a design on the narrow paper, using watercolors with brushes or cotton swabs.
2. After the paper dries, the teacher will staple the end of the painted paper to the end of a straw, at a 90-degree angle to the straw.
3. The adult will roll the paper tightly around the straw and fasten it with a rubber band.
4. The paper will be allowed to set overnight.
5. Next day, each child will take the rubber band off his or her adding machine tape and play with the resulting Chinese yo-yo.

Note: This is a two-day project.

4

Adhesive Tape Prints

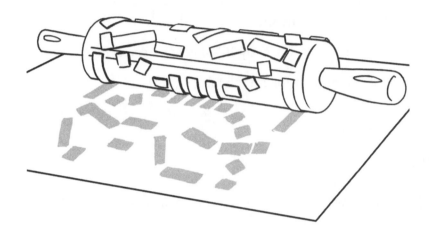

DEVELOPMENTAL GOALS:

- ✂ To enhance creativity
- ✂ To develop muscle control

LEARNING OBJECTIVE:

Using rolling pins, foam insulation tape, trays, paper towels, tempera paint, and paper or foil, the child will roll designs across paper.

MATERIALS:

Rolling pins—one for each color used
Self-adhesive foam insulation tape (purchased at hardware store)
Large foam trays or cookie sheets
Paper towels
Two or three colors of tempera paint
Construction paper or aluminum foil
Newspaper
Dish soap

ADULT PREPARATION:

1. Cut insulation tape into different lengths.
2. Stick tape on each rolling pin to make a desired pattern. (Pattern should go all the way around the rolling pin.)
3. Make a paint blotter (see "Helpful Hints," page xi).

PROCEDURES:

The child will complete the following steps:

1. Roll the rolling pin across the paint blotter, covering all the insulation tape with paint.
2. Roll the rolling pin across paper.
3. Repeat steps 1 and 2 with other colors.

Aluminum Foil Art

AGES: 2–5

DEVELOPMENTAL GOALS:

✂ To develop eye-hand coordination

✂ To improve fine motor control

LEARNING OBJECTIVE:

Using aluminum foil, cotton swabs, small brushes, an egg carton, and tempera paint, the child will paint on a different medium.

MATERIALS:

Aluminum foil
Cotton swabs or small brushes
Foam egg carton or small containers
Tempera paint
Dish soap

ADULT PREPARATION:

1. Mix paint with dish soap.

2. Put four to six colors of paint into individual cups of foam egg carton or small containers.

3. Cut aluminum foil in 8" by 10" sheets for each child.

4. Put the aluminum foil on the table or easel.

PROCEDURES:

1. The child will use cotton swabs or small brushes to apply paint to the aluminum foil.

Note: This may be used as wrapping paper.

Apple Prints

AGES: 1–5

DEVELOPMENTAL GOALS:

- ✂ To follow directions
- ✂ To observe the pattern of apple seeds

LEARNING OBJECTIVE:

Using a stamp pad, foam plate, liquid coloring, paper, and an apple, the child will make apple prints.

MATERIALS:

Foam shoe insert
Foam plate or tray
Liquid watercolor
Paper
Apple
Knife
Scissors

ADULT PREPARATION:

1. Cut apple in half horizontally; star-shaped seed pattern will be visible.
2. Allow apple to sit approximately 20 minutes to dry out.
3. Make a stamp pad (see "Helpful Hints," page xi).
4. Cut paper to desired size.

PROCEDURES:

The child will complete the following steps:

1. The child will press apple half onto stamp pad.
2. The child will press color-coated apple half onto paper.
3. The child will repeat steps 1–2 to make additional apple prints.

B

AGES: 4–5

DEVELOPMENTAL GOALS:

- To coordinate large and small muscles
- To observe a transfer of color

LEARNING OBJECTIVE:

Using a paper bag, marbles, tempera paint, water, and spoons, the child will paint inside a bag.

MATERIALS:

Paper bag (lunch- or grocery-size)
Marbles or jingle bells
Several colors of tempera paint
Several small cups
Spoons
Water
Scissors
Masking tape

Bag Painting

ADULT PREPARATION:

1. Put tempera paint in small cups, one color per cup.
2. Mix tempera paint with water to watercolor consistency.
3. Put a marble (or jingle bell) into each cup.

PROCEDURES:

The child will complete the following steps:

1. Use spoons to get one marble of each color.
2. Drain excess paint from the spoon before dropping the marble in the bag. (If too much paint is poured into the bag, the bag may weaken and tear.)
3. Hold the bag closed at the top and shake it so that the marbles or bells roll around and paint the inside of the bag.
4. Cut the sides of bag with scissors to allow drying.

ACTIVITY SUGGESTIONS:

When the paper is dry, it may be cut to form a Thanksgiving vest, or it may be used for holiday wrapping paper.

SAFETY PRECAUTION:

Marbles and jingle bells may present a choking hazard. This activity requires direct supervision. Younger children may do this activity if the teacher is the only one to handle the marbles or jingle bells. The teacher may also seal the bag shut with masking tape before the child shakes it.

Balloon Painting

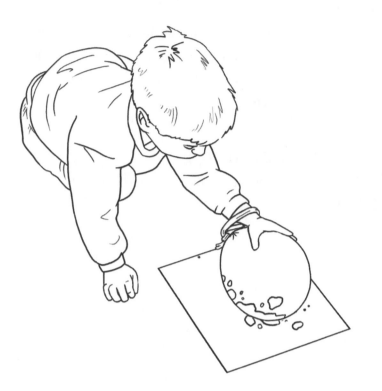

ADULT PREPARATION:

1. Cut off foot-to-calf portion of panty hose (or leave knee-high stockings intact).

2. Insert a balloon into the foot section of the panty hose or knee-high stocking.

3. Blow up a balloon inside the panty hose (one balloon for each color of paint).

4. Tie a knot in the balloon, then tie a knot in the stocking, securing the balloon inside. (Creating a holder for the balloon ensures that if it pops, it will not endanger the child.)

5. Tie the excess (calf portion) of the stocking in a loop to make a handle for the child to slip one hand through.

6. Make a paint blotter for each color of paint (see "Helpful Hints," page xi).

continued

AGES: 1–5

DEVELOPMENTAL GOALS:

✂ To stimulate arm muscles

✂ To delight in movement

LEARNING OBJECTIVE:

Using a small balloon, knee-high stockings, paper, and tempera paint, the child will paint with a balloon.

MATERIALS:

Balloon—small
Panty hose or knee-high stockings
Paper
Tempera paint
Dish soap
Plate or pan for paint
Paper towels

Balloon Painting continued

PROCEDURES:

The child will complete the following steps:

1. Place the balloon on the paint blotter.
2. Press the stocking-covered balloon onto the paper.
3. Repeat steps 1–2 with other colors.

 SAFETY PRECAUTION:

Balloons may present a choking hazard. This activity requires direct supervision.

Baseball Painting

ADULT PREPARATION:

1. Pour a small amount of tempera paint on the plate.

2. Mix paint with dish soap.

3. Cut paper to fit the box or bucket.

4. Put paper in the box or bucket.

PROCEDURES:

The child will complete the following steps:

1. Roll a baseball through the paint.

2. Place the ball on the paper inside the box or bucket.

3. Roll the ball around, leaving a paint trail.

4. Repeat steps 1–3 with other colors.

AGES: 1–5

DEVELOPMENTAL GOALS:

- ✂ To develop motor control
- ✂ To improve problem-solving abilities

LEARNING OBJECTIVE:

Using a baseball, tempera paint, and a box, the child will paint by rolling a ball.

MATERIALS:

Baseball
Tempera paint
Dish soap
Plate
Box or bucket with lid
Paper
Scissors

Bean Mosaic

AGES: 3–5

DEVELOPMENTAL GOALS:

✂ To develop eye-hand coordination

✂ To improve fine motor skills

LEARNING OBJECTIVE:

Using dried beans, glue, cotton swabs, and heavy paper, the child will create a bean mosaic.

MATERIALS:

Variety of dried beans
School glue
Heavy paper or cardboard
Milk bottle cap or small container
Cotton swabs or small brushes
Small bowl

ADULT PREPARATION:

1. Pour glue into milk bottle cap or small container.

2. Put beans in small bowl.

PROCEDURES:

The child will complete the following steps:

1. Use a cotton swab or small brush to spread glue on paper or cardboard.

2. Place beans on the paper or cardboard.

Note: For younger children, use a smaller piece of paper and a larger brush to spread the glue; this will accommodate their shorter attention span.

⚠ SAFETY PRECAUTION:

This activity requires close supervision, because the beans may present a choking hazard.

Berry Basket Prints

AGES: 3–5

DEVELOPMENTAL GOALS:

- ✂ To experience rhythm
- ✂ To feel competent in motor control

LEARNING OBJECTIVE:

Using strawberry baskets, tempera paint, construction paper, and a wooden block, the child will make berry basket prints.

MATERIALS:

Pint-size strawberry baskets
Tempera paint
Plate or tray
Dish soap
Paper towel
Construction paper
Wooden block

ADULT PREPARATION:

1. Make a separate paint blotter for each color used (see "Helpful Hints," page xi).

PROCEDURES:

The child will complete the following steps:

1. Press bottom of strawberry basket into paint blotter.
2. Press bottom of basket onto construction paper.
3. Pound block into the basket to ensure that paint from all areas of the basket is pressed onto the paper.
4. Remove basket.
5. Repeat steps 1–3 with other colors, using a separate strawberry basket for each color.

EXPANSION:

Finger paint berries on the basket design.

Bingo Bottle Prints

AGES: 1–5

DEVELOPMENTAL GOALS:

✂ To enjoy movement

✂ To coordinate large and small muscles

LEARNING OBJECTIVE:

Using bingo bottles, diluted tempera paint, and paper, the child will make small, circular prints.

MATERIALS:

Bingo bottles (may be purchased from discount or school supply stores)

Tempera paint

Water

Paper

ADULT PREPARATION:

1. Dilute tempera paint with water (two parts paint, one part water).
2. Fill bingo bottles with diluted tempera paint.

PROCEDURES:

The child will complete the following steps:

1. Paint with strokes or make dots on paper with the bingo bottles.

Notes: Bingo bottles filled with washable ink may be purchased instead of filling empty bottles with diluted paint. (Be sure the ink is washable.)

This activity may be done at an easel or table.

ACTIVITY SUGGESTIONS:

Use the bingo bottles to make fruit on a tree or spots on an animal.

Block Prints

ADULT PREPARATION:

1. Make a paint blotter for each color of paint. (see "Helpful Hints," page xi).

PROCEDURES:

The child will complete the following steps:
1. Press the block into the paint.
2. Press the block onto the paper.
3. Repeat steps 1–2.

ACTIVITY SUGGESTIONS:

Block painting may be used to create a brick pattern for a house during a family unit, or it can be used to create Humpty Dumpty's wall during a Mother Goose unit.

AGES: 2–5

DEVELOPMENTAL GOALS:

✄ To develop eye-hand coordination

✄ To distinguish shapes

LEARNING OBJECTIVE:

Using blocks, tempera paint, paper towels, and construction paper, the child will make block prints.

MATERIALS:

Tempera paint
Paper towels
Plate or tray
Dish soap
Blocks of wood (different sizes and shapes—at least one for each color of paint)
Construction paper

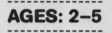

AGES: 2–5

DEVELOPMENTAL GOALS:

- ✄ To foster creativity
- ✄ To develop and coordinate large and small muscles

LEARNING OBJECTIVE:

Using a broom, dustpan, paint, and paper, the child will apply paint to paper in a sweeping motion.

MATERIALS:

Tempera paint
Dish soap
Toy broom and dustpan
Paper
Plastic covering for floor

Broom and Dustpan Painting

ADULT PREPARATION:

1. Mix tempera paint with dish soap.
2. Put a small amount of the paint mixture into the dustpan.
3. Lay plastic covering on the floor.
4. Tape paper to the plastic floor covering.

PROCEDURES:

The child will complete the following steps:

1. Dip the broom into the dustpan.
2. Sweep paint across the paper.

Note: This activity can be done outside.

Bubble Art

AGES: 3–5

DEVELOPMENTAL GOALS:

- ✄ To develop muscular coordination through the use of a straw
- ✄ To follow directions

LEARNING OBJECTIVE:

Using pie pans, water, detergent, liquid coloring, plastic straws, and paper, the child will create paint-filled bubbles that adhere to paper.

MATERIALS:

Pie pans
Water
Joy® dish detergent (other dish soaps do not work)
Food coloring or liquid watercolor
Plastic straws
Paper
Push pin

® The Procter & Gamble Company. Used by permission.

ADULT PREPARATION:

1. Fill pie pans half full with water.
2. Add approximately one-fourth cup Joy® detergent to each pan.
3. Add food coloring or liquid watercolor to make a deep hue.
4. Poke a hole through the straw about one-fourth of the way down from the top of the straw. This will ensure that the child cannot suck the paint up through the straw but will still be able to blow through the straw.
5. Make certain the child knows how to blow through a straw.

PROCEDURES:

The child will complete the following steps:

1. Blow through a straw, making bubbles in the pan until the pan is nearly overflowing with bubbles.

continued

Bubble Art continued

2. Lay paper across the pan on top of the bubbles, popping the colorful bubbles onto the paper.

3. Repeat steps 1–2 with other colors.

Notes: The paper should be large enough to overlap the sides of the pan. If it is too small, the child will dip the paper into the pan instead of laying it across the pan.

Younger children may do this activity if the teacher or adult blows the bubbles. Children may need assistance in placing the paper on top of the bubbles.

Bubble Wrap Prints

AGES: 1–5

DEVELOPMENTAL GOALS:

- ✂ To enhance sensory stimulation through use of a new texture
- ✂ To develop motor control

LEARNING OBJECTIVE:

Using plastic bubble wrap, a foam sponge-brush, tempera paint, and paper, the child will create a series of circular prints.

MATERIALS:

Plastic bubble wrap (one piece for each color used)
Sponge brush or foam roller brush (one for each color)
Tempera paint
Dish soap
Container, plate, or small tray
Large tray
Paper
Scissors
Masking tape

ADULT PREPARATION:

1. Mix tempera paint with dish soap in container, plate, or tray.
2. If using a foam roller brush, paint needs to be in a plate or tray for easier access.
3. Cut a piece of bubble wrap material for each color of paint used. The bubble wrap should be cut to match the size of the paper.
4. Tape the bubble wrap material to the table or large tray, bubble side up.
5. Place sponge brush or foam roller brush in paint.

PROCEDURES:

The child will complete the following steps:

1. Roll paint onto the bubble wrap.
2. Place paper over the bubble wrap.
3. Rub a hand over the paper, ensuring that the paint adheres to the paper.

continued

19

Bubble Wrap Prints continued

4. Carefully lift the paper to see the design.
5. Repeat steps 1–4 if using different colors.

ACTIVITY SUGGESTION:

During an outer space unit, cut the paper into a circle. The print will resemble craters on the moon.

Bull's-Eye

ADULT PREPARATION:

1. Pour sand into the foot of stocking. The amount of sand depends on the size of the children involved, because they should be able to handle the stocking "sandbags" easily.

2. Tie end of stocking to ensure that sand does not leak out. Make one for each color to be used.

3. Put tempera paint on small tray or plate. Mix with dish soap.

4. Cut paper to fit inside box.

5. Put paper in box and place the box on the floor, or cover the floor with plastic and put paper directly on the plastic.

PROCEDURES:

The child will complete the following steps:

1. Press a sandbag into the paint.

2. Hold the sandbag over the box and drop the bag onto the paper inside the box. (The paint will make a starburst design on the paper.)

3. Repeat steps 1–2 with other colors, using a different sandbag for each color.

Notes: It is important to place the paper in a box or lay the paper on the floor covered with plastic, because the paint will splatter.
This activity may be done outside.

ACTIVITY SUGGESTION:

Use fluorescent paint on black construction paper to create comets or starbursts.

DEVELOPMENTAL GOALS:

✄ To express emotions through art

✄ To improve large muscle development

LEARNING OBJECTIVE:

Using sand, panty hose or knee-high stockings, tempera paint, a box, and paper, the child will drop paint onto paper.

MATERIALS:

Panty hose or knee-high stockings
Tempera paint (fluorescent, if possible)
Dish soap
Small tray or plate
Sand, grits, rice, or birdseed
Box with high sides
Paper
Plastic covering for floor

Bundle Art

DEVELOPMENTAL GOALS:

✄ To develop the muscles in the hands, wrists, and arms

✄ To delight in movement

LEARNING OBJECTIVE:

Using crayons, markers, rubber bands, a small toy car, and paper, the child will transport color onto paper.

MATERIALS:

Crayons or markers
Rubber bands
Small toy car
Paper

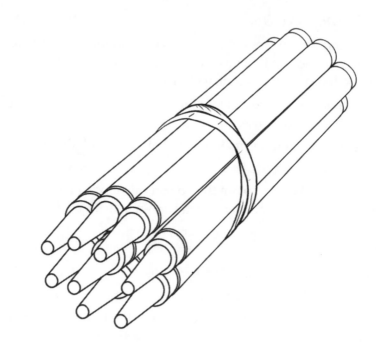

ADULT PREPARATION:

1. Gather various colors of crayons or markers into a bundle that will fit inside a child's fist or on the back of a small toy car.

2. Secure the bundle with a rubber band.

PROCEDURES:

The child will complete the following steps:

1. Draw with the bundle of crayons, or "drive" the crayons across the paper by securing the bundle on the back of the toy car and then pushing the car, leaving a trail of colors.

22

Cake Painting

AGES: 2–5

DEVELOPMENTAL GOALS:

- ✄ To stimulate the sense of smell
- ✄ To enjoy a new art form

LEARNING OBJECTIVE:

Using cake mixture, squeeze bottles (or plastic resealable freezer bags), liquid coloring, and cardboard, the child will create a scented design.

MATERIALS:

White cake mix
Water
Oil
Mixing bowl
Small bowls
Squeeze bottles or resealable plastic freezer bags (one for each color used)
Liquid watercolor or food coloring
Cardboard or tag board
Scissors

ADULT PREPARATION:

1. Prepare cake mix in a large bowl according to directions, but omit the eggs.
2. Separate the mix into smaller bowls.
3. Add a different color of liquid watercolor or food coloring to each bowl and mix well.
4. Put the colored cake mix into squeeze bottles or plastic freezer bags.
5. If using plastic bags, snip one corner so the bag resembles a baker's icing bag.
6. Cut cardboard or tagboard to desired size.

PROCEDURES:

The child will complete the following steps:

1. Squeeze variously colored cake mix onto cardboard to make designs.
2. Smell the batter, and attempt to describe the scent.
3. Allow two days to dry.

continued

Cake Painting continued

Note: Younger children have more success using squeeze bottles than plastic bags.

⚠ **SAFETY PRECAUTION:**

All of the ingredients are edible since the egg has been removed from the recipe. However, if the batter is left to sit prior to use, make sure it is refrigerated.

Carrot Painting

AGES: 1–5

DEVELOPMENTAL GOALS:

- ✂ To improve eye-hand coordination
- ✂ To use a familiar object in a new way
- ✂ To develop fine motor control

LEARNING OBJECTIVE:

Using whole carrots, tempera paint, and water, the child will paint with a new medium.

MATERIALS:

Whole carrots with green stem attached
Orange tempera paint
Green tempera paint
Water
Small containers

ADULT PREPARATION:

1. Pour different colors of tempera paint into separate containers.
2. Dilute paint with water, three parts paint to one part water.

PROCEDURES:

The child will complete the following steps:

1. Place the carrot stem into paint.
2. Brush color onto the paper, using the green stem of the carrot like a paintbrush and the carrot itself as a handle.

VARIATION:

Use sliced or baby carrots in the same manner that acorns were used in Acorn Painting (see page 2).

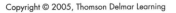

25

Cereal Mosaic

AGES: 1–5

DEVELOPMENTAL GOALS:

✂ To stimulate the senses with textures

✂ To develop small muscles

LEARNING OBJECTIVE:

Using cereal, diluted glue, a brush, and heavy paper, the child will create a mosaic.

MATERIALS:

Variety of cereal
Bowls (one for each cereal used)
Glue
Water
Brush
Tag board or heavy paper
Scissors
(Optional) Glitter

ADULT PREPARATION:

1. Dilute glue with water (two parts glue, one part water).
2. Sort cereal into bowls.
3. Cut tag board or heavy paper to desired size.

PROCEDURES:

The child will complete the following steps:

1. Brush glue onto paper.
2. Glue the cereal onto paper.
3. (Optional) Drizzle glue onto the cereal and then shake glitter onto the wet glue. Shake off excess glitter.

Note: Children may do step 2 of adult preparation.

Chalk Shaving Art

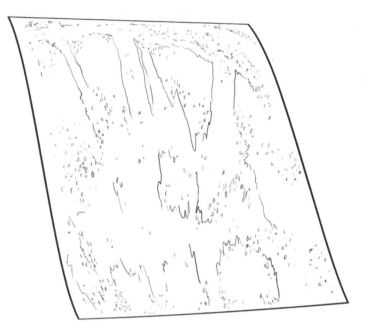

DEVELOPMENTAL GOALS:

- ✂ To observe a transformation
- ✂ To develop eye-hand coordination

LEARNING OBJECTIVE:

Using a pan, water, wire colander, colored chalk, and paper, the child will create a new art form.

MATERIALS:

Pan
Water
Wire colander or grease screen
Colored chalk (bright colors look best)
Paper

ADULT PREPARATION:

1. Fill pan one-third full with water.
2. Place colander over water.

PROCEDURES:

The child will complete the following steps:

1. Scrape chalk against colander. (Chalk shavings will fall onto surface of water.)
2. Place paper gently in water.
3. Lift paper out of water. Chalk shavings will adhere to paper.

continued

Chalk Shaving Art continued

Notes: If pan is bumped, chalk shavings may fall to the bottom of the pan. The chalk will not adhere to the paper if this happens. The water may need to be changed after several children have participated.

VARIATION:

The child may complete the following steps instead:

1. Brush diluted glue (two parts glue to one part water) onto paper.
2. Place the colander over the paper.
3. Scrape the chalk against the colander. Chalk shavings will fall onto the paper and adhere to it.

Comb and Brush Art

ADULT PREPARATION:

1. Make a paint blotter for each color of paint (see "Helpful Hints," page xi).

PROCEDURES:

The child will complete the following steps:

1. Press the comb or brush onto the paint blotter.
2. Run the comb or brush across the paper.
3. Repeat steps 1–2 with different colors.

AGES: 1–5

DEVELOPMENTAL GOALS:

- ✂ To develop creativity
- ✂ To use objects in a new way

LEARNING OBJECTIVE:

Using a comb, brush, tempera paint, and paper, the child will paint with familiar objects.

MATERIALS:

Tempera paint (colors may be used to match the children's hair)
Dish soap
Foam plate
Paper towels
Small comb and brush
Paper

29

Corn Syrup Painting

DEVELOPMENTAL GOALS:

- ✄ To experience a new art form
- ✄ To stimulate muscles

LEARNING OBJECTIVE:

Using light corn syrup, liquid coloring, wide brushes, and heavy paper, the child will create a hard, shiny design.

MATERIALS:

Light corn syrup
Food coloring or liquid watercolors
Cups or small containers
Wide brushes
Heavy paper
Spoons

ADULT PREPARATION:

1. Pour corn syrup in cups.
2. Add food coloring or liquid watercolors.
3. Stir with a spoon to mix the coloring and corn syrup.

PROCEDURES:

The child will complete the following steps:

1. Paint on heavy paper.
2. Hang or lay on plastic to dry overnight. (This dries to a hard, shiny finish.)

Notes: If paintings are hung to dry, syrup that drips will harden and be difficult to remove from the floor, so cover beneath the drawings with newspaper.

Do not lay corn syrup drawings directly on newspaper, because they will stick to the newspaper. Instead, lay them on a drying rack or plastic.

If the weather is damp, allow two days to dry.

This is a fun and tasty experience!

Cotton Ball Painting

ADULT PREPARATION:

1. Attach a cotton ball to the end of each clothespin.
2. Mix tempera paint with dish soap on plate or tray.

PROCEDURES:

The child will complete the following steps:

1. Dip cotton ball into paint.
2. Spread paint on paper.
3. Use a separate cotton ball for each color of paint.

VARIATION:

The child may dip a cotton ball into dry (powdered) paint and rub the cotton across the paper, which will have a pastel effect.

C

DEVELOPMENTAL GOALS:

✄ To delight in movement

✄ To stimulate grasping muscles

LEARNING OBJECTIVE:

Using a variety of papers and tempera paint colors, the child will make prints.

MATERIALS:

Newsprint, wrapping paper, construction paper or copier paper
Tempera paint
Dish soap
Tray or plate

Crumpled Paper Prints

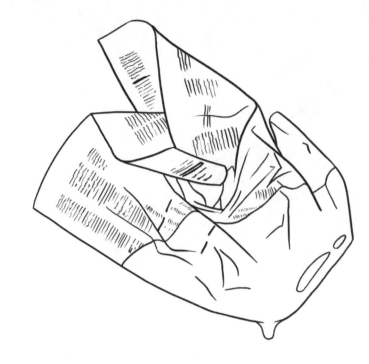

ADULT PREPARATION:

1. Pour paint onto tray or plate; mix with dish soap.
2. Crumple different papers into balls, making one ball for each paint color.

PROCEDURES:

The child will complete the following steps:

1. Dip the ball of paper into the paint.
2. Press the ball onto the paper.
3. Repeat steps 1–2 with a different color or type of balled paper.

Note: Different types of paper change the types of prints achieved.

32

Damp Paper Painting

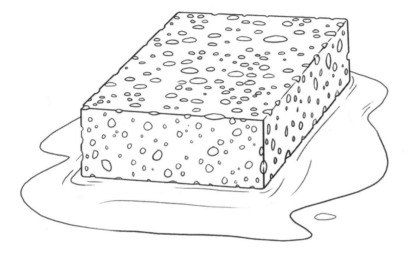

AGES: 1–5

DEVELOPMENTAL GOALS:

✂ To improve self-help skills

✂ To develop color recognition

LEARNING OBJECTIVE:

Using a sponge, water, dry tempera paints, shaker containers, and glossy finger paint paper, the child will experience a new art form.

MATERIALS:

Glossy finger paint paper
Sponge
Water
Bowl
Dry tempera paint
Shaker containers

ADULT PREPARATION:

1. Put an assortment of dry tempera colors into shaker containers.
2. Place water in the bowl.
3. Dip a sponge in the bowl, then squeeze out the excess water.

PROCEDURES:

The child will complete the following steps:

1. Using the sponge, spread a very thin layer of water onto the finger paint paper.
2. Shake various colors of dry tempera onto the damp paper.
3. Identify the colors used when asked.
4. Allow paper to dry.

Note: Children may be able to do step 3 of adult preparation.

VARIATION:

This may be an outside activity during warm weather.

Dental Floss Painting

AGES: 2–5

DEVELOPMENTAL GOALS:

✁ To become familiar with a tool that promotes dental health

✁ To develop fine motor control

LEARNING OBJECTIVE:

Using dental floss, tempera paint, and paper, the child will create a unique painting.

MATERIALS:

Dental floss
White tempera paint
Dish soap
Container
Paper (darker colors work best)

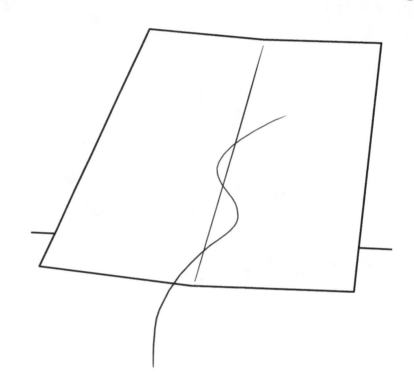

ADULT PREPARATION:

1. Put white tempera paint in container. Mix with dish soap.
2. Tear or cut pieces of dental floss approximately 12 inches long.
3. Fold paper in half.
4. Open paper to lay flat.

PROCEDURES:

The child will complete the following steps:

1. Dip dental floss into white tempera paint.
2. Lay the floss on half of the paper, leaving one end of the floss hanging outside the paper.
3. Fold the other half of the paper over the floss.
4. Hold the paper closed with one hand, while slowly pulling the floss out of the folded paper with the other.
5. Unfold the paper to see the design.
6. Repeat steps 1–6.

continued

Dental Floss Painting continued

Notes: The adult may need to assist with steps 3 and 4 of the procedures.

The dental floss may be tied to a clothespin; the clothespin will hang outside of the paper. The child will hold the clothespin to pull the dental floss; this permits easier handling for a young child or one with special needs.

VARIATIONS:

Yarn may be used instead of floss. Younger children may find yarn easier to hold than floss.

Other colors of paint may be substituted.

D

DEVELOPMENTAL GOALS:

- ✂ To develop creativity
- ✂ To enhance eye-hand coordination

LEARNING OBJECTIVE:

Using a doily, paper, tempera paint, and roller brush, the child will make prints.

MATERIALS:

Doily (one for each child)
Paper
Tempera paint
Dish soap
Masking tape
Roller brush or sponge
Foam tray or plate
Paper towels

Doily Prints

ADULT PREPARATION:

1. Tape the doily (putting the tape on the solid part of the doily) on the paper with masking tape.
2. Make a paint blotter (see "Helpful Hints," page xi).

PROCEDURES:

The child will complete the following steps:

1. Roll roller brush or place sponge on the paint blotter.
2. Go over the entire doily with the roller or sponge, making sure to fill in all the holes with paint.
3. Carefully pick up doily, revealing the print.

**Notes: Children may need assistance with step 3 of the procedures. Doilies usually tear and can be used only once.
This can be done at the easel or art table.**

ACTIVITY SUGGESTIONS:

Use a heart-shaped doily for Valentine's Day or a shamrock doily for St. Patrick's Day.

Drizzle Art

ADULT PREPARATION:

1. Pour tempera paint into small containers. Use a separate container for each color.
2. Dilute paint with water (two parts water, one part paint).

PROCEDURES:

The child will complete the following steps:

1. Dip a brush or craft stick into one color of paint.
2. Hold the brush or craft stick over paper and drizzle the paint onto the paper.
3. Repeat with different colors, using a separate brush or craft stick.

Note: The more color the child uses, the brighter the picture. Encourage the child to drizzle in all directions.

DEVELOPMENTAL GOALS:

- ✄ To improve fine motor control
- ✄ To delight in the use of color

LEARNING OBJECTIVE:

Using diluted tempera paint, brushes, and paper, the child will drizzle paint onto paper.

MATERIALS:

Paper
Tempera paint
Water
Paintbrushes or craft sticks,
Small containers

Dye Painting

DEVELOPMENTAL GOALS:

- ✂ To experience a new art form
- ✂ To stimulate muscle development

LEARNING OBJECTIVE:

Using cabbage water, coffee, brushes, and paper, the child will paint with another medium.

MATERIALS:

Purple cabbage
Water
Pan
Stove
Containers
Coffee
White paper or cloth
Brushes (at least one for each color)
Knife to cut cabbage

ADULT PREPARATION:

1. Cut purple cabbage into chunks.
2. Boil in two quarts of water until the water turns purple.
3. Pour the tinted water into a container and let cool.
4. Brew instant or regular coffee.
5. Pour the coffee into a separate container and let cool.

PROCEDURES:

The child will complete the following steps:

1. Use cool cabbage water and coffee as watercolors, brushing them onto white paper or cloth.

38

Egg Roll

AGES: 2–5

ADULT PREPARATION:

1. Mix paint with dish soap and a small amount of water (two parts water, one part paint, one-quarter part soap).
2. Place boiled eggs in paint containers.
3. Cut paper to fit in box or bucket.
4. Place paper in the box or bucket.

PROCEDURES:

The child will complete the following steps:

1. Remove egg with a spoon and place on the paper.
2. Roll egg in the box or bucket by tipping the container from side to side.
3. Repeat with other colors.

Notes: Use a bucket with a lid for younger children.

Plastic eggs may be used instead of boiled eggs.

 SAFETY PRECAUTION:

If using boiled eggs, children must wash hands with soap and water after handling eggs.

DEVELOPMENTAL GOALS:

- ✂ To promote problem solving
- ✂ To coordinate large and small muscles

LEARNING OBJECTIVE:

Using boiled eggs, diluted tempera paint, spoons, a box, and paper, the child will roll paint across the paper.

MATERIALS:

One boiled egg for each color
Box or bucket with lid
Tempera paint
Water
Dish soap
Paper
Spoons (one for each color of paint)
Containers (one for each color of paint)
Scissors

E

Eggshell Mosaic

AGES: 2–5

DEVELOPMENTAL GOALS:

✂ To foster creativity

✂ To improve fine motor skills

LEARNING OBJECTIVE:

Using eggshells, glue, and paper, the child will create a mosaic.

MATERIALS:

Eggshells
Resealable plastic bag
Food coloring or liquid watercolor
Rubbing alcohol
Newspaper or paper towels
Glue
Paper

ADULT PREPARATION:

1. Clean eggshells thoroughly, then air dry.
2. Color eggshells (see "Helpful Hints," page xii) and let dry.

PROCEDURES:

The child will complete the following steps:

1. Glue eggshells onto paper in different designs.

Notes: Children may help to color the eggshells.

This is a two-day procedure; the eggshells must be prepared a day in advance.

⚠ SAFETY PRECAUTION:

Wash hands with soap and water after handling eggshells.

Egg Yolk Painting

ADULT PREPARATION:

1. Put egg yolk in paint container.
2. Mix with liquid coloring.

PROCEDURES:

The child will complete the following steps:
1. Use brush to paint egg yolk mixture on paper.
2. Allow to dry (this leaves a shiny finish).

Note: When adding coloring to the yellow yolk, the color will be altered (for example, adding blue coloring to the yellow yolk will make green).

 ## SAFETY PRECAUTION:

Supervise children closely to prevent the ingestion of raw egg yolk. Children should wash their hands with soap when they are through painting with egg yolk.

AGES: 2–5

DEVELOPMENTAL GOALS:

- ✂ To observe a transformation of colors by mixing them
- ✂ To foster creativity

LEARNING OBJECTIVE:

Using egg yolk, food coloring, brushes, and paper, the child will paint with a different medium.

MATERIALS:

Food coloring or liquid watercolor
Egg yolks
Paint containers
Brushes
Paper

Eyedropper Painting

AGES: 3–5

DEVELOPMENTAL GOALS:

✄ To develop eye-hand coordination

✄ To stimulate the growth of small muscles

LEARNING OBJECTIVE:

Using liquid watercolor, eyedroppers, coffee filters, and paper towels, the child will drip color, watching as it is absorbed by the filter.

MATERIALS:

Coffee filters (one for each child)
Paper towels or newspaper
Eyedroppers
Liquid watercolor (assorted colors)
Small containers
Trays

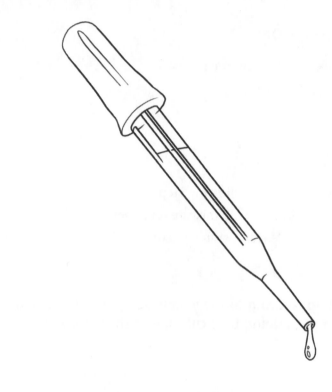

ADULT PREPARATION:

1. Fill small containers with liquid watercolor using a separate container and eyedropper for each color.

2. Cover trays with paper towels or newspaper.

3. Lay coffee filter on each tray.

PROCEDURES:

The child will complete the following steps:

1. Fill eyedropper with liquid watercolor.

2. Squirt color onto filter.

3. Watch as the color is absorbed by the filter and spreads through it.

4. Repeat with different colors.

continued

Eyedropper Painting continued

EXPANSION:

Place a piece of paper under the coffee filter. The design will be absorbed by both the filter and the paper, giving the child two products.

VARIATION:

Instead of the eyedropper, use a paintbrush, cotton swab, or small squeeze bottle.

43

F

Feather Duster Painting

AGES: 1–5

DEVELOPMENTAL GOALS:

- ✄ To delight in movement
- ✄ To participate in a new art experience

LEARNING OBJECTIVE:

Using feather dusters, tempera paint, and paper, the child will paint with a new object.

MATERIALS:

Feather duster (one for each color of paint)
Tempera paint (two or three colors)
Dish soap
Foam trays or plates
Paper towels
Paper

ADULT PREPARATION:

1. Make a paint blotter (see "Helpful Hints," page xi).

PROCEDURES:

The child will complete the following steps:

1. Brush the duster through the paint.
2. Brush the duster across the paper.
3. Repeat with other colors.

Note: Rinse all paint from the feather duster when finished, then let it air-dry.

Fingerpainting

AGES: 1–5

DEVELOPMENTAL GOALS:

- ✂ To express emotions through art
- ✂ To promote sensory stimulation

LEARNING OBJECTIVE:

Using finger paint, paper, and a tray, the child will spread paint with his or her hands and then transfer it to paper.

MATERIALS:

Finger paint
Paper
Serving tray or cookie sheet
Spoons

ADULT PREPARATION:

1. Spoon desired amount of finger paint onto tray.

PROCEDURES:

The child will complete the following steps:

1. Spread paint with fingers or hands.
2. Lay paper over the painted tray (with adult's help) and press with hands.
3. Watch as adult carefully lifts paper to uncover the original design, now transferred to the paper.

VARIATION:

Finger paint on bubble wrap, then follow steps 2–3.

DEVELOPMENTAL GOALS:

- ✂ To follow directions
- ✂ To increase muscle strength

LEARNING OBJECTIVE:

Using soda bottles, tempera paint, and paper, the child will make flower prints.

MATERIALS:

2-liter soda bottles
20-ounce soda bottles with caps
Various colors of tempera paint
Dish soap
Tray or plate
Paper towels
Paper

Flower Prints with Soda Bottles

ADULT PREPARATION:

1. Make a paint blotter (see "Helpful Hints," page xi).

PROCEDURES:

The child will complete the following steps:

1. Press the bottom of 2-liter bottle onto a paint blotter.
2. Press the 2-liter bottle's bottom onto paper.
3. Turn the 20-ounce bottle over and press its cap into a paint blotter of a different color.
4. Press painted cap into the center of the 2-liter bottle-bottom print. (The effect resembles a flower.)

Flower Smashing

AGES: 2–5

DEVELOPMENTAL GOALS:

✄ To delight in rhythm and movement

✄ To relieve tension

LEARNING OBJECTIVE:

Using flowers, paper, a block of wood, and newspaper, the child will smash flowers to leave a print on paper.

MATERIALS:

Colorful live flowers such as pansies (some lawn-care services will donate flowers that they are replacing at the end of the season)

Two sheets of white construction paper per child

Block of wood

Newspaper

ADULT PREPARATION:

1. Place a thick pad of newspaper on the table to soften the noise.
2. Put two sheets of white paper on the newspaper.
3. Place flowers between the sheets of white paper.

PROCEDURES:

The child will complete the following steps:

1. Pound the flowers between the sheets of paper, using the block.
2. Remove the top sheet of paper to see the colored design made by the flowers.

Note: The child may do steps 2–3 of the preparation.

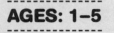

F

AGES: 1–5

DEVELOPMENTAL GOALS:

✂ To foster creativity

✂ To enhance large muscle development

LEARNING OBJECTIVE:

Using flyswatters, tempera paint, and paper, the child will make prints.

MATERIALS:

Flyswatters (one for each color of paint)
Tempera paint
Dish soap
Foam plates
Paper towel blotter
Paper
Plastic covering or newspaper

Flyswatter Painting

ADULT PREPARATION:

1. Make a paint blotter (see "Helpful Hints," page xi).
2. Lay flyswatter flat on the blotter.
3. Place plastic covering or newspaper on the table and/or floor.

PROCEDURES:

The child will complete the following steps:

1. Swat the paper with the flyswatter, or press the flyswatter gently onto the paper to make a print.
2. Repeat with different colors.

continued

48

Flyswatter Painting continued

Notes: The child may be allowed to do step 3 of preparation by swatting the paint blotter with the flyswatter.

Flyswatters may be purchased with unique patterns, such as a butterfly pattern or a handprint.

VARIATION:

This activity may be done with the paper placed inside a box or on an easel, or the activity may be done outside.

F

AGES: 2–5

DEVELOPMENTAL GOALS:

- ✄ To improve fine motor control
- ✄ To use familiar objects in a new way

LEARNING OBJECTIVE:

Using forks, tempera paints, and paper, the child will make prints.

MATERIALS:

Variously sized forks
Tempera paint
Dish soap
Paper towel
Small tray or plate
Paper

Fork Prints

ADULT PREPARATION:

1. Make a paint blotter (see "Helpful Hints," page xi).

PROCEDURES:

The child will complete the following steps:

1. Press the forks into the paint blotter.
2. Press the forks onto the paper.
3. Repeat with different colors.

Fruit Prints

ADULT PREPARATION:

1. Cut fruit pieces in half and allow to dry (see "Helpful Hints," page xii).
2. Make a stamp pad using a foam shoe insert (see "Helpful Hints," page xi).

PROCEDURES:

The child will complete the following steps:

1. Press fruit on stamp pad.
2. Press fruit on paper.

Note: Fruit needs to air dry so paint will adhere to it.

AGES: 2–5

DEVELOPMENTAL GOALS:

✂ To follow directions
✂ To experience a new art form

LEARNING OBJECTIVE:

Using fruit, a foam shoe insert, liquid coloring, and paper, the child will create a fruit print.

MATERIALS:

Fruit (apples or oranges)
Foam shoe insert
Plastic lid or foam plate
Food coloring or liquid watercolor
Paper

G

DEVELOPMENTAL GOALS:

- ✄ To stimulate the sense of smell
- ✄ To develop eye-hand coordination

LEARNING OBJECTIVE:

Using gelatin, brushes, and paper, the child will paint with a new medium.

MATERIALS:

Several colors of
    powdered gelatin
Boiling water
Small containers
Small brushes
Paper

Gelatin Painting

ADULT PREPARATION:

1. Mix gelatin with water according to the package directions.
2. Set on counter to cool. *Do not refrigerate*.
3. Pour into small containers.
4. Lay paper on table or at easel.

PROCEDURE:

1. The child will paint with gelatin and small brushes.

Notes: If gelatin starts to thicken, set container in a pan of warm water to reliquefy.

This is a sticky project but smells wonderful!

Glove Painting

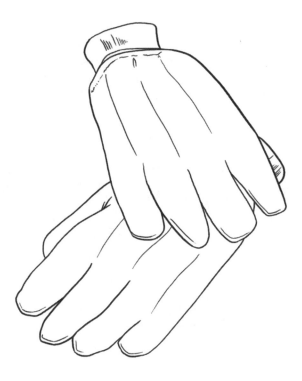

AGES: 1–5

DEVELOPMENTAL GOALS:

- ✄ To stimulate muscle development
- ✄ To delight in movement

LEARNING OBJECTIVE:

Using gloves, tempera paint, and paper, the child will paint wearing a glove.

MATERIALS:

Gloves of various sizes and textures
Tempera paint
Dish soap
Foam plate or tray
Paper towel
Paper

ADULT PREPARATION:

1. Make a paint blotter (see "Helpful Hints," page xi).

PROCEDURES:

The child will complete the following steps:

1. Put on glove.
2. Lay gloved hand on paint blotter.
3. Press gloved hand onto paper.

ACTIVITY SUGGESTIONS:

During a gardening unit, use brown paint with a gardening glove. For a winter unit, use white paint with a mitten.

Glue Trails

DEVELOPMENTAL GOALS:

- ✂ To develop patience
- ✂ To observe the transformation of objects through movement

LEARNING OBJECTIVE:

Using glue, liquid coloring, squirt bottles, and paper plate, the child will move colored glue around the plate.

MATERIALS:

White school glue
Liquid watercolors or food coloring
Paper plate or paper
Small squirt bottle

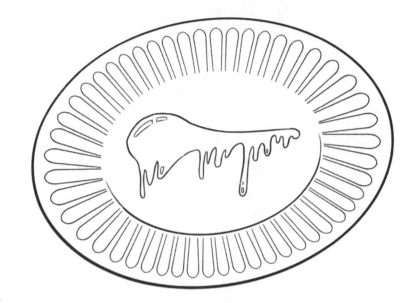

ADULT PREPARATION:

1. Put liquid watercolor or food coloring in a small squirt bottle. The bottle must also have a small opening to limit the amount of coloring used.

PROCEDURES:

The child will complete the following steps:

1. Squirt a quarter-size amount of glue in the center of the paper plate. The amount may vary according to the size of plate or paper.

2. Squirt one drop each of two or three different hues of food coloring or liquid watercolor onto the spot of glue.

3. Slowly tilt the plate, watching the glue and coloring as they run together, leaving a trail across the plate.

54

Golf Ball Painting

AGES: 1–5

DEVELOPMENTAL GOALS:

✂ To move objects rhythmically

✂ To enhance large muscle development

LEARNING OBJECTIVE:

Using golf balls, diluted tempera paint, an ice cream bucket, and paper, the child will roll paint around the paper.

MATERIALS:

Golf balls
Water
Tempera paint
Small containers
Spoons
Ice cream buckets
Paper

ADULT PREPARATION:

1. Cut paper into a circle to fit in the bottom of the ice cream bucket.
2. Mix one part tempera paint with one part water in small container.
3. Place paper in the ice cream bucket.
4. Put golf balls into tempera paint of different colors.

PROCEDURES:

The child will complete the following steps:

1. **Younger child:** Watch as the adult uses a spoon to drain excess paint from one of the golf balls and to place it on the paper inside the ice cream bucket. **Older child:** Using a spoon, drain excess paint from one of the golf balls and place it on the paper inside the ice cream bucket.
2. **Younger child:** With adult assistance, put the lid on the bucket, then shake the bucket. **Older child:** Gently roll the ball across the paper by tilting the bucket.
3. Replace ball in the paint and repeat with a different color.

VARIATION:

The golf ball may be replaced with balls of other types and sizes.

55

Grits Mosaic

AGES: 2–5

DEVELOPMENTAL GOALS:

- ✂ To develop self-help skills
- ✂ To stimulate fine motor skills

LEARNING OBJECTIVE:

Using grits, glue, and heavy paper, the child will create a mosaic of grits.

MATERIALS:

Grits (uncooked)
Food coloring
Container with lid, or resealable plastic bag
Glue
Heavy paper
Bowls
Paintbrush

ADULT PREPARATION:

1. Stain uncooked grits several different colors (see "Helpful Hints," page xii).
2. Place stained grits in bowls.
3. Pour glue into separate bowl.
4. Place paintbrush and paper on table.

PROCEDURES:

The child will complete the following steps:
1. Drizzle or spread glue with paintbrush on paper.
2. Sprinkle grits of different colors on glue.
3. Gently shake off excess.
4. Allow to dry.

Notes: Grits may also be used in other activities, instead of glitter.

This is a two-day process. Color the grits one day; use the tinted grits the next day. The child may help with preparation.

Gumdrop Sculptures

AGES: 3–5

DEVELOPMENTAL GOALS:

- ✂ To increase creativity
- ✂ To develop eye-hand coordination

LEARNING OBJECTIVE:

Using gumdrops and toothpicks, the child will create a sculpture.

MATERIALS:

Large and small gumdrops
Colored toothpicks
Foam or paper plates
Large resealable plastic bags

ADULT PREPARATION:

1. Place toothpicks and gumdrops of different sizes and colors on the child's plate.

PROCEDURES:

The child will complete the following steps:

1. Arrange a sculpture of gumdrops and toothpicks by poking one end of a gumdrop with a toothpick and then connecting it to other gumdrops with toothpicks.

2. Place sculpture in a large resealable plastic bag to carry it home.

Note: Be sure to provide extra gumdrops to eat.

continued

Gumdrop Sculptures continued

SAFETY PRECAUTION:

Close supervision is necessary. Gumdrops may present a choking hazard; toothpicks may also be a safety concern.

ACTIVITY SUGGESTION:

During an outer space unit, the gumdrop sculptures may resemble robots or constellations.

Handprints

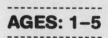

DEVELOPMENTAL GOALS:

✂ To follow directions

✂ To feel a sense of accomplishment

LEARNING OBJECTIVE:

Using hands, paintbrushes, tempera paint, and paper, the child will create prints.

MATERIALS:

Paintbrushes
Tempera paint
Dish soap
Container
Paper

ADULT PREPARATION:

1. Put tempera paint into a container.
2. Add dish soap to the paint and mix well.

PROCEDURES:

The child will complete the following steps:

1. Paint one entire hand with a brush. (This enables the paint to go on more evenly. If the hand is dipped into paint instead, the effect is a blob rather than a handprint.)
2. Press painted hand onto paper.
3. Repeat steps 1–2.

Notes: Have a bucket of warm soapy water available for quick cleanup.

Younger children will need assistance painting their hands.

continued

Handprints continued

ACTIVITY SUGGESTIONS:

✄ The handprints with fingers pointed up to the top of the paper become trees, sails on a boat, turkeys, Indians, or flowers.

✄ The handprints with fingers pointed down towards the bottom of the paper can become ghosts or spiders.

✄ The handprints with fingers lying horizontally can become flags or fish.

✄ If pressed around a circle, palms on the circle, fingers away from the circle, the handprints become a wreath. Fingerprints may be added for holly berries.

Hats

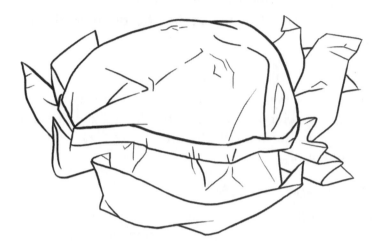

DEVELOPMENTAL GOALS:

✄ To interact with an adult

✄ To create a new art form

LEARNING OBJECTIVE:

Using newspaper, masking tape, diluted tempera paint, spray bottles, glue, and feathers, stickers, or other decorations, the child will create a hat.

MATERIALS:

Newspaper
Masking tape
Diluted tempera paint
Small spray bottles
Tissue paper, feathers, stickers, or other decorations
Glue

ADULT PREPARATION:

1. Take two whole sheets of newspaper and lay one diagonally on top of the other.
2. Place the two newspaper sheets on child's head. Hold in place with hand flat on top of child's head (adult 1).
3. Wrap masking tape on the newspaper, completely around the child's head at the hairline (adult 2).
4. Beginning at the front, roll the newspaper up to the tape, making a brim all the way around the hat (adults 1 and 2).
5. Put diluted tempera paint into spray bottles (either or both adults).

PROCEDURES:

The child will complete the following steps:

1. Spray paint the hat.
2. When hat is dry, decorate it with feathers, tissue paper, glue, stickers, or other decorations.

continued

GLUE

Hats continued

Notes: This activity requires two adults to assist in making the newspaper hat. Each hat is individually fitted to the child's head. The child's creativity is exercised in decorating the hat.

Younger children may have difficulty sitting still long enough for adults to wrap the masking tape around their heads.

Some children may not like having their heads covered with newspaper.

VARIATION:

Instead of using spray bottles and paint, mix ½ cup of evaporated milk with liquid watercolor until it reaches the desired hue. The child will brush the milk mixture onto the hat which leaves the hat with a smooth, hard finish.

ACTIVITY SUGGESTIONS:

During a baseball unit, children may make ball caps by placing the paper off center on the child's head. Let more newspaper hang over the child's face, then roll the paper so the excess on the front resembles the bill on a baseball player's cap. A cowboy hat may be made during a wild west unit by rolling the length longer on the sides, and then leaving the front and back of the hat shorter.

Horseshoe Prints

AGES: 2–5

DEVELOPMENTAL GOALS:

- ✂ To develop creativity
- ✂ To stimulate muscle growth

LEARNING OBJECTIVE:

Using horseshoes, tempera paint, brushes, and paper, the child will create horseshoe prints.

MATERIALS:

Toy horseshoes or real ones
Tempera paint
Dish soap
Brushes
Containers
Paper or newsprint

ADULT PREPARATION:

1. Put tempera paint in containers.
2. Add dish soap and mix well.

PROCEDURES:

The child will complete the following steps:

1. Paint the horseshoe, using a brush.
2. Place the painted side of the horseshoe down on the paper to make a print. Or place the paper on top of the horseshoe and, holding the paper still, rub a hand over the horseshoe to make a print.
3. Repeat with paint of other colors.

Horsetail Painting

AGES: 2–5

DEVELOPMENTAL GOALS:

✂ To delight in rhythmic movement

✂ To coordinate large and small muscles

LEARNING OBJECTIVE:

Using yarn or discarded doll hair, rubber bands or spring clothespins, tempera paint, and paper, the child will paint using a new tool.

MATERIALS:

Yarn or discarded doll hair

Rubber bands or spring clothespins

Small containers of tempera paint

Water

Paper

ADULT PREPARATION:

1. Cut yarn into a dozen strands, each approximately six inches long, or use doll hair. If using doll hair, use 4–6 inch lengths of hair, bunched into a ¼" to 1" diameter.

2. Gather strands together to resemble a horsetail, using a rubber band or clothespin.

3. Dilute two parts tempera paint with one part water, mixing it in small containers.

PROCEDURES:

The child will complete the following steps:

1. Dip the "horsetail" into paint.

2. Paint with the horsetail by swishing it back and forth across the paper.

Ice Painting

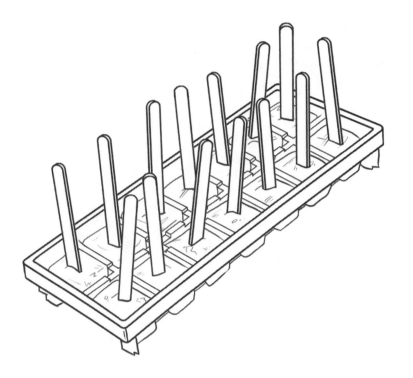

DEVELOPMENTAL GOALS:

- ✂ To observe a transformation
- ✂ To develop small muscles

LEARNING OBJECTIVE:

Using ice cubes frozen on craft sticks, dry tempera paint, and paper, the child will paint with different materials.

MATERIALS:

Muffin tin or
  ice cube tray
Water
Craft sticks
Dry tempera paint
Paper
Tray

ADULT PREPARATION:

1. Put water in muffin tin or ice cube tray.
2. Put one craft stick in each section of the muffin tin or tray. The craft stick will lay at an angle.
3. Freeze overnight, making ice pops.
4. Loosen ice pops in muffin tin or tray.
5. Place muffin tin or tray with frozen ice pops on table.
6. Place paper in tray.

PROCEDURES:

The child will complete the following steps:

1. Sprinkle dry tempera paint on paper.
2. Rub ice pop over the tempera powder.
3. Ice will melt, and tempera will liquefy, creating a painting.

continued

Ice Painting continued

Note: This may also be done in the water or sensory table.

VARIATION:

Add liquid watercolor to water before freezing, then allow the child to use the frozen watercolor, on a craft stick, to paint.

Imprints

ADULT PREPARATION:

1. Ask children to gather leaves, twigs, acorns, or other items from nature.
2. Pour plaster of Paris into bowl.
3. Add water and mix according to directions on box.
4. Spoon mixture onto foam plate.

PROCEDURES:

The child will complete the following steps:

1. Rub one side of leaf, twig, or acorn lightly with petroleum jelly.
2. Press the leaf or other nature object into plaster of Paris, petroleum jelly side down.
3. Repeat with other nature objects.
3. Allow the mixture to harden.
4. Carefully remove leaves, twigs, acorns, or other objects. Imprinted designs will be visible in the plaster.

DEVELOPMENTAL GOALS:

- ✄ To experience a new art form
- ✄ To observe a transformation

LEARNING OBJECTIVE:

Using plaster of Paris mixture, a plate, and items from nature, the child will create an imprint.

MATERIALS:

Plaster of Paris
Water
Bowl
Spoon
Petroleum jelly
Foam plates
Leaves
Twigs
Acorns

Jelly Bean Painting

AGES: 3–5

DEVELOPMENTAL GOALS:

✂ To enjoy a sense of rhythm

✂ To coordinate large and small muscles

LEARNING OBJECTIVE:

Using jelly beans, diluted tempera paint, spoons, a tray, and paper, the child will paint in a new way.

MATERIALS:

Jelly beans (real or plastic)

Tray (older child) or ice cream bucket with lid (younger child)

Small containers

Tempera paint

Water

Spoons

Paper

ADULT PREPARATION:

1. Mix one part water with one part tempera paint in small containers.
2. Place paper in bottom of ice cream bucket (for younger child) or on tray (for older child).
3. Put jelly beans into diluted tempera paint.

PROCEDURES:

The **younger child** will complete the following steps:

1. Watch as the adult picks up jelly beans from the paint with a spoon, drains excess paint from the jelly beans, and puts them on the paper at the bottom of an ice cream bucket.
2. With adult assistance, put the lid on the bucket and then shake the bucket, allowing the jelly beans to cover the paper with paint.

The **older child** will complete the following steps:

1. Pick up jelly beans from the paint with a spoon.
2. Drain excess paint from the jelly beans.
3. Put jelly beans on the paper in the tray.
4. Carefully tilt the tray, allowing the jelly beans to move, leaving a trail of paint on the paper.

⊘ SAFETY PRECAUTION:

Jelly beans may present a choking hazard. For younger children, only the teacher handles the jelly beans. Supervision is required.

VARIATION:

Use jingle bells during a holiday unit instead of jelly beans.

Jump Painting

AGES: 3–5

DEVELOPMENTAL GOALS:

- ✂ To practice a new art form
- ✂ To enhance large muscle development

LEARNING OBJECTIVE:

Using squirt bottles, tempera paint, construction paper, and paper clips, the child will spread paint by jumping on the paper.

MATERIALS:

Small squirt bottles
Tempera paint
Dish soap
Large-size construction paper (two per child)
Paper clips
Large sheet of plastic

ADULT PREPARATION:

1. Put tempera paint in squirt bottles. Mix with dish soap.
2. Lay a large sheet of plastic on the ground or floor.
3. Place one sheet of large construction paper on top of the plastic.
4. Squirt tempera on the paper, away from the edges.

PROCEDURES:

The child will complete the following steps:

1. Lay another sheet of paper on top of the painted sheet.
2. Watch as the adult paper clips the two sheets of paper together.
3. Jump on the paper, spreading the paint.

Note: This activity can be done outside instead of inside, eliminating the need for plastic covering on the floor.

continued

Jump Painting continued

⚠ SAFETY PRECAUTION:

The child may be allowed to squirt the paint onto the bottom sheet of paper. This requires very close supervision, however, because if too much paint is used, the top sheet of paper and the child will slide when the child jumps on the top sheet of paper. If you are doing this activity inside, make sure to hold the child's hands during the jumping. This will help prevent sliding.

Key Prints

AGES: 2–5

DEVELOPMENTAL GOALS:

- ✄ To develop eye-hand coordination
- ✄ To enhance fine motor control

LEARNING OBJECTIVE:

Using keys, clothes-pins, washable inkpads, and paper, the child will create key prints.

MATERIALS:

Keys
Hot glue gun
Small spools or spring clothespins
Paper
Foam shoe inserts
Liquid watercolors or food coloring

ADULT PREPARATION:

1. With glue gun, attach a small spool or clothespin to the flat side of each key, creating a handle.
2. Make stamp pads in different colors (see "Helpful Hints," page xi).

PROCEDURES:

The child will complete the following steps:

1. Holding the key by the handle, press the key into the stamp pad.
2. Press the key onto the paper.
3. Repeat steps 2–3 with stamp pads of different colors.

Kicking Rubber Band Ball Painting

AGES: 2–5

DEVELOPMENTAL GOALS:

✂ To develop creativity

✂ To coordinate large and small muscles

LEARNING OBJECTIVE:

Using kicking rubber band balls, tempera paint, and paper, the child will paint with a new type of object.

MATERIALS:

Kicking rubber band balls (one for each color of paint)
Tempera paint
Dish soap
Plate or tray
Paper

ADULT PREPARATION:

1. Make paint blotters in several different colors (see "Helpful Hints," page xi).

PROCEDURES:

The child will complete the following steps:

1. Press a kicking rubber band ball on the paint blotter.
2. Press the ball on the paper several times.
3. Repeat, using paint of different colors.

ACTIVITY SUGGESTION:

Use fluorescent paint on black paper to resemble fireworks or stars.

Kitchen Prints

AGES: 1–5

DEVELOPMENTAL GOALS:

✂ To use familiar objects in a new way

✂ To follow directions

LEARNING OBJECTIVE:

Using kitchen utensils, paint blotter, and paper, the child will make prints.

MATERIALS:

Tempera paint
Dish soap
Paper towels
Foam plate or tray
Paper
Potato mashers, cookie cutters, jar or plastic lids, spatulas, or other kitchen utensils

ADULT PREPARATION:

1. Make a paint blotter (see "Helpful Hints," page xi).

PROCEDURES:

The child will complete the following steps:

1. Press potato masher or other kitchen utensil onto paint blotter.

2. Press utensil onto paper.

3. Repeat with other items.

Lace Prints

DEVELOPMENTAL GOALS:

✂ To experience a new art form

✂ To encourage creativity

LEARNING OBJECTIVE:

Using lace, roller brushes, tempera paint, and paper, the child will create lace prints.

MATERIALS:

Flat, wide, lace in different patterns, cut into different lengths
Roller brushes
Tempera paint
Dish soap
Containers
Paper

ADULT PREPARATION:

1. Put one color of paint in each container used. Mix with dish soap.
2. Cut lace into various lengths.
3. Fold paper in half.

PROCEDURES:

The child will complete the following steps:

1. Paint lace in several lengths with a roller brush, using tempera paint of several colors.
2. Open the folded paper and lay the painted lace on one side of paper.
3. With adult help, fold the other side of the paper over the lace and press the top of the paper down onto the lace.
4. Lift top half of paper and remove the lace.
5. Repeat steps 1–4 with different colors.

Laminating Film Art

ADULT PREPARATION:

1. Pour tempera paint into small containers. Mix with dish soap.
2. Cut used portions of laminating film into desired shapes.

PROCEDURE:

1. Using a cotton swab or small brush, the child will apply paint to the film.

ACTIVITY SUGGESTIONS:

After the film dries, a picture frame may be placed around it to create a suncatcher. Laminating film may also be stapled into a cylinder shape with streamers attached, to form a windsock.

AGES: 2–5

DEVELOPMENTAL GOALS:

- ✂ To use new materials
- ✂ To develop fine motor control

LEARNING OBJECTIVE:

Using laminating film, cotton swabs, and tempera paint, the child will paint on a different type of surface.

MATERIALS:

Scraps of laminated film
Cotton swabs or small
   brushes
Tempera paint
Dish soap
Small containers

Leaf Prints

AGES: 1–5

DEVELOPMENTAL GOALS:

✄ To work with others

✄ To appreciate nature

LEARNING OBJECTIVE:

Using leaves, tempera paint, brushes, and a rolling pin, the child will create leaf prints.

MATERIALS:

Tempera paint
Dish soap
Containers
Brushes
Rolling pin
Fresh leaf (a dried leaf would break)
Paper (two sheets per child)

ADULT PREPARATION:

1. Put tempera paint into containers.
2. Mix paint with dish soap.

PROCEDURES:

The child will complete the following steps:

1. Paint the entire leaf with a brush.
2. Lay the leaf between two sheets of paper.
3. Roll a rolling pin over the top sheet of paper.
4. Lift off the top paper to see the leaf print.

VARIATION:

Paint the leaf with cotton swabs, using fall colors.

76

Magnet Art

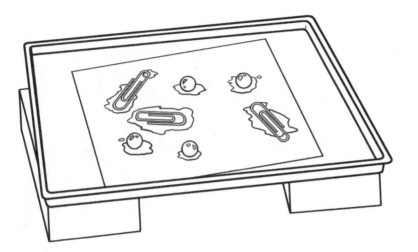

ADULT PREPARATION:

1. Mix two parts tempera paint and one part water.
2. Add several of the magnetic marbles to each container of diluted paint.
3. Prop pan on two large blocks, putting one at each end and leaving the center of the pan free so that a child's hands will fit underneath it.
4. Put a sheet of paper on the pan.

PROCEDURES:

The child will complete the following steps:

1. Spoon several magnetic marbles onto paper on the pan after draining excess paint from the spoon.
2. Take the magnetic wand and drag it across the bottom of the pan to move the paint-covered marbles across the paper, leaving a trail of paint.

 SAFETY PRECAUTION:
Use close supervision to ensure that small children do not put the marbles into their mouths.

AGES: 2–5

DEVELOPMENTAL GOALS:

✂ To observe magnetic properties
✂ To develop muscle coordination

LEARNING OBJECTIVE:

Using magnetic marbles, a magnet wand, diluted tempera paint, spoons, paper, a metal pan, and two large blocks, the child will paint in a new way.

MATERIALS:

Magnet wand
Magnetic marbles
Paper
Small containers
Spoons
Several colors of tempera paint
Water
Metal pan cookie sheet or plastic tray
Two large wooden blocks

Marbling

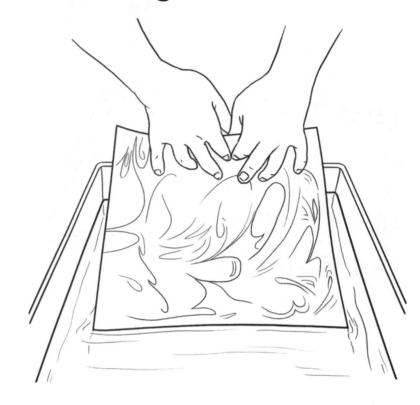

AGES: 2–5
(Younger children
may require
more assistance.)

DEVELOPMENTAL GOALS:

- ✂ To develop creativity
- ✂ To increase motor control

LEARNING OBJECTIVE:

Using vegetable oil, dry tempera paint, a pan, water, spoons, and paper, the child will create a marbling effect on paper.

MATERIALS:

Vegetable oil
Several colors of dry
  tempera paint
Small containers
Spoons
Pan
Water
Paper

ADULT PREPARATION:

1. Fill small containers one-fourth full of oil.
2. Add one heaping spoonful of a different color of powdered paint to each container and stir until mixed well.
3. Fill pan one-third full of water.

PROCEDURES:

The child will complete the following steps:

1. Drizzle a spoonful of each color of oil and paint mixture onto the top of the water in the pan, without mixing the colors into the water.
2. Lay the paper on top of the water. (Do not press it down to the bottom.)
3. Carefully lift paper from the water, revealing the marbled effect.

Note: The adult will need to change the water when it becomes muddy with the mixed colors.

Marshmallow Painting

ADULT PREPARATION:

1. Place marshmallows on sticks or straws, creating a handle for each marshmallow.
2. Pour liquid watercolors into small containers.
3. Put marshmallows with handles beside watercolor containers.
4. Lay paper on the table.

PROCEDURES:

The child will complete the following steps:

1. Holding a marshmallow by its handle, dip it into the watercolor.
2. Spread watercolor across the paper, using the marshmallow as a brush.
3. Use the marshmallow as a stamp, making circular prints on the paper.
4. Repeat with different colors.
5. When asked, identify the colors used.

Notes: After being dipped into the color several times, the marshmallows may become gooey and slide off the craft stick. They will need to be replaced, so be sure to have lots of marshmallows with handles available.

 SAFETY PRECAUTION:

Marshmallows may be used with younger children only with strict supervision, because they have been associated with choking in young children.

VARIATION:

Place small marshmallows in a resealable plastic bag. Add dry tempera paint. Seal the bag and shake; the dry powdered paint will adhere to the marshmallows. Then use the marshmallows to make a collage. The marshmallows may also be used to make fruit on a tree or blossoms in the spring.

ACTIVITY SUGGESTION:

During a winter unit, the marshmallows may be glued on construction paper to resemble snow or snowmen.

AGES: 3–5

DEVELOPMENTAL GOALS:

✂ To identify colors
✂ To improve fine muscle skills

LEARNING OBJECTIVE:

Using marshmallows, sticks, liquid watercolors, and paper, the child will paint with different objects.

MATERIALS:

Large marshmallows
Craft sticks or plastic straws
Liquid watercolors
Small containers
Paper

Mask

AGES: 2–5

DEVELOPMENTAL GOALS:

✄ To delight in accomplishment

✄ To experience a new art form

LEARNING OBJECTIVE:

Using heavy paper, a tongue depressor, glue, sequins, glitter, feathers, and stickers, the child will create a mask.

MATERIALS:

Tag board or poster board
Glue
Scissors
Spray paint
Stapler
Tongue depressor
Sequins, glitter, feathers, stickers, and so on, for decorations

ADULT PREPARATION:

1. Place the child's hands palms down on a sheet of paper, with thumbs together and fingers extended.

2. Trace the child's hands on the paper.

3. Cut out the shape drawn on the paper.

4. Cut eyes inside each palm.

5. Spray paint the resulting mask.

6. Staple tongue depressor at right angle to one end of the mask, so that the child can hold the mask in front of his or her face by using the tongue depressor as a handle.

PROCEDURE:

1. The child will glue sequins, glitter, and/or other decorations onto the mask.

continued

Mask continued

Note: If the child's handprints are too small to make a mask or to cut adequate eyeholes, the teacher's hands may be traced for the mask.

VARIATION:

Instead of using the child's handprints to make a mask, the teacher may cut out the handle portion of a plastic gallon milk carton, leaving 3 inches on each side. Then the adult cuts circles for eyes on each side of the handle. Next the adult spray paints the mask. When the paint dries, the child may decorate their mask.

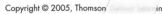

Masking Tape Art

DEVELOPMENTAL GOALS:

- ✄ To improve self-help skills
- ✄ To develop fine motor control

LEARNING OBJECTIVE:

Using masking tape, construction paper, a brush, and tempera paint, the child will experience a new method of painting.

MATERIALS:

Masking tape
Construction paper
Wide brush or roller brush
Tempera paint
Dish soap
Foam tray or plate

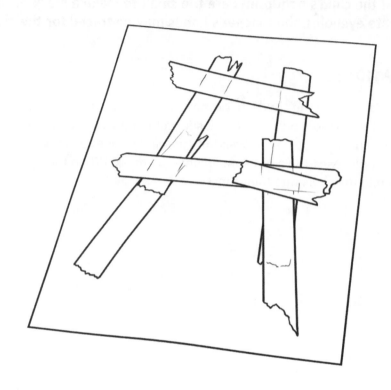

ADULT PREPARATION:

1. Pour tempera paint onto foam tray or plate.
2. Mix paint with dish soap.
3. Tear off strips of masking tape.

PROCEDURES:

The child will complete the following steps:

1. Stick masking tape on paper in a desired design or in the shape of a letter.
2. Using a wide brush or roller, paint over the entire paper.
3. With adult help, peel off the tape while the paint is still wet, to uncover design.

continued

Masking Tape Art continued

Notes: Be sure to remove the tape while the paint is still wet, because tape is difficult to remove once the paint is dry, even though painter's masking tape is easier to remove than other tape.

Use smaller sheets of paper for two-year-olds, to accommodate their shorter attention span.

ACTIVITY SUGGESTIONS:

Use the masking tape to create stripes on the flag. Masking tape art may also be used to make lines on the paper to resemble a baseball or football field.

Milk Painting

DEVELOPMENTAL GOALS:

✂ To develop creativity

✂ To stimulate eye-hand coordination

LEARNING OBJECTIVE:

Using milk, liquid coloring, brushes, and paper, the child will create a pastel painting.

MATERIALS:

Evaporated milk, whole milk, or half-and-half
Small containers
Food coloring or liquid watercolors
Brushes or cotton swabs
Paper
Spoons
Can opener (for evaporated milk)

ADULT PREPARATION:

1. Pour milk into small containers.
2. Add food coloring or liquid watercolor to milk and stir well. Add the amount of watercolor needed to achieve the desired hue.

PROCEDURES:

The child will complete the following steps:

1. Paint on the paper, using brushes or cotton swabs with the milk-based paint.
2. Set aside to dry. The milk product will leave a shiny, odorless finish.

84

Necklace

ADULT PREPARATION:

1. Cut yarn long enough to make a necklace.
2. Wrap a small strip of masking tape around the end of the yarn to make an aglet, or dip the end of the yarn into glue. **If glue is used, set aside to dry overnight.**
3. Tie a noodle to the opposite end of the yarn so the pasta noodles will not slide off as child threads them onto the end with the aglet.

PROCEDURE:

1. The child will use an aglet to thread pasta noodles onto yarn.

Note: After the child has strung pasta noodles on the yarn, tie the finished necklace to make it the desired size.

VARIATION:

Instead of pasta noodles, use plastic straws cut into pieces, cereal, or construction paper cutouts.

AGES: 2–5

DEVELOPMENTAL GOALS:

- ✂ To follow directions
- ✂ To encourage the growth of small muscles

LEARNING OBJECTIVE:

Using yarn, masking tape, glue, and dyed pasta noodles, the child will create a necklace.

MATERIALS:

Yarn
Masking tape or glue
Dyed pasta noodles (see "Helpful Hints," page xii)

Netting Prints

DEVELOPMENTAL GOALS:

- ✂ To delight in movement
- ✂ To express emotions

LEARNING OBJECTIVE:

Using birdseed, uncooked rice, netting, stamp pad, and paper, the child will create prints.

MATERIALS:

Birdseed or
  uncooked rice
Netting
Foam shoe insert
Water
Liquid watercolor or
  food coloring
Foam tray or plate
Paper

ADULT PREPARATION:

1. Put birdseed or rice into netting.
2. Tie off netting or secure with a rubber band.
3. Make a stamp pad (see "Helpful Hints," page xi).

PROCEDURES:

The child will complete the following steps:

1. Press netting filled with birdseed or rice onto the stamp pad.
2. Place net on paper.
3. Repeat steps 1–2.

VARIATION:

Use a small aquarium net to make the prints. Press the empty net on the stamp pad, and then press the net onto the paper.

Noodle Painting

AGES: 3–5

DEVELOPMENTAL GOALS:

- ✂ To promote creativity
- ✂ To improve small muscle skills

LEARNING OBJECTIVE:

Using pasta noodles, a fork, diluted tempera paint, and paper, the child will paint with a different object.

MATERIALS:

Long pasta noodles (cooked and cooled)
Fork
Tempera paint
Water
Dish soap
Foam tray
Paper towel
Paper

ADULT PREPARATION:

1. Cook, rinse, and cool long pasta noodles. (If noodles are prepared a day in advance, they should be stored in the refrigerator.)
2. Make a paint blotter.

PROCEDURES:

The child will complete the following steps:

1. Pick up noodles with fork.
2. Dip noodles into paint.
3. Lay the dipped noodles on paper.
4. Drag and twirl the colored pasta over the paper.
5. Repeat steps 1–4.

Note: Noodles of a different thickness can be used to add variety.

continued

N

Noodle Painting continued

VARIATION:

Divide cooked and drained (but not rinsed) spaghetti into large reseal-able plastic bags. Add food coloring or liquid watercolor and shake until the color is distributed evenly. Keep refrigerated until needed. Then have the child lay the noodles on a piece of paper to create a design. The noodles will adhere to the paper when dry.

ACTIVITY SUGGESTION:

Prepare spaghetti as noted in "Variation" section, but do not add color. Lay the spaghetti on a sheet of black paper or waxed paper. Add a plastic spider to make a web, as part of a Halloween unit.

Nose Painting

DEVELOPMENTAL GOALS:

- ✂ To promote creative expression
- ✂ To enhance self-esteem

LEARNING OBJECTIVE:

Using paint mixture, cotton swabs, a mirror, easel, and paper, the child will paint with his or her nose.

MATERIALS:

Mirror
Liquid tempera paint (three or four colors)
Foam tray or plate
Cotton swabs
Dish soap
Hand lotion
Diaper wipes
Paper
Easel

ADULT PREPARATION:

1. Put a small amount of tempera paint on a plate or tray. Use at least 2 or 3 separate spots of color on the plate, resembling an artist's palette.
2. Mix each spot of paint separately with a squirt of dish soap and a squirt of lotion. Do not mix the colors.
3. Tape paper to the easel.

PROCEDURES:

The child will complete the following steps:

1. Looking into the mirror, use a cotton swab to paint the end of nose. (May use more than one swab and paint nosetip several different colors. Use a different swab for each color to avoid mixing the colors.)
2. Go to the easel and rub painted nose on the paper.
3. Repeat steps 1–2.

continued

Nose Painting continued

Notes: Adult should offer treated wipes to wipe nose clean after each trip to the easel and should offer assistance when necessary. Children need to learn to take turns. There is one mirror, and usually one easel in a classroom. At times the easel may be double sided. Once again, as stated in the preface, instructions are for one child, also in the preface/or helpful hints is the number of children for art activities according to their age.

Nuts and Bolts

ADULT PREPARATION:

1. Pour tempera paint of several different colors into small containers.
2. Dilute two parts paint with one part water, mixing well with a spoon until paint becomes the consistency of watercolor.
3. Put nuts and bolts into diluted paint of different colors.
4. Cut paper to fit inside the ice cream bucket.
5. Place paper into empty ice cream bucket.

PROCEDURES:

The child will complete the following steps:

1. Pick up nuts and bolts from the paint with a spoon.
2. Drain excess paint from the spoon, then spoon the nuts and bolts onto the paper.
3. With adult assistance, place the lid on the bucket.
4. Shake the bucket, moving the painted nuts and bolts across the paper.
5. Repeat steps 1–4.

SAFETY PRECAUTION:

This activity requires constant supervision, because nuts and bolts present a choking hazard for young children and should not be put into their mouths.

DEVELOPMENTAL GOALS:

✄ To enjoy rhythm and movement
✄ To coordinate large and small muscles

LEARNING OBJECTIVE:

Using nuts and bolts, diluted tempera paint, spoons, paper, and a bucket, the child will paint with loose hardware.

MATERIALS:

Nuts and bolts
Small containers
Tempera paint
Water
Spoons
Paper
Empty ice cream
    bucket with lid
Scissors

Oatmeal Art

AGES: 1–5

DEVELOPMENTAL GOALS:

- ✄ To stimulate the senses through texture
- ✄ To improve gluing techniques

LEARNING OBJECTIVE:

Using oatmeal, diluted glue, brushes, a spoon, and paper, the child will create a textured art project.

MATERIALS:

Oatmeal
Paper
Glue
Small containers
Water
Paintbrushes
Spoon

ADULT PREPARATION:

1. Pour one part glue and one part water into a small container.
2. Mix well with a spoon.
3. Pour oatmeal into a bowl.

PROCEDURES:

The child will complete the following steps:
1. Spread diluted glue on the paper with a brush.
2. Using a spoon and/or hands, put oatmeal on the glue.
3. Shake off excess oatmeal.

ACTIVITY SUGGESTION:

Glue oatmeal on black or dark blue paper during a winter unit to simulate a snowstorm.

Oil Art

AGES: 3–5

DEVELOPMENTAL GOALS:

- ✂ To follow directions
- ✂ To create a new art form

LEARNING OBJECTIVE:

Using cooking oil, wax paper, cotton ball, tissue paper, and construction paper, the child will experience a new art form.

MATERIALS:

Vegetable oil
Wax paper
Cotton ball
Tissue paper or construction paper
Scissors
Small plastic or foam plate

ADULT PREPARATION:

1. Pour small amount of oil on plate.
2. Cut tissue paper or construction paper into desired shapes and sizes.
3. Tear off a sheet of wax paper approximately 8–12 inches long.
4. Fold wax paper in half, creasing the fold.

PROCEDURES:

The child will complete the following steps:

1. Open the folded wax paper.
2. Using a cotton ball, put oil on the wax paper, on one side of the fold line.
3. Place tissue paper or construction paper shapes on the oiled half of the wax paper.

continued

Oil Art continued

4. Fold over the other half of wax paper, securing the tissue paper or construction paper between the folded sides of the sheet of wax paper.

ACTIVITY SUGGESTION:

Use as a suncatcher.

Oilcan Painting

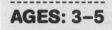
DEVELOPMENTAL GOALS:

✂ To develop cognitive growth through the use of new materials

✂ To stimulate muscle development

LEARNING OBJECTIVE:

Using oilcans, diluted tempera paint, paper, and a box, the child will paint with different tools.

MATERIALS:

Oilcans
Tempera paint
Water
Paper
Box
Scissors

ADULT PREPARATION:

1. Dilute several tempera paint colors with water to the consistency of water.
2. Put thinned tempera paint into oilcans.
3. Cut paper to fit inside box.
4. Put paper into a box (to eliminate wayward squirts).

PROCEDURE:

The child will complete the following steps:

1. Squirt paint onto paper by pumping the oilcan.
2. Repeat step 1, using other colors.

Note: Liquid watercolors may be used instead of diluted tempera paints.

VARIATION:

Paper may be hung outside on a fence or laid on the ground, with a hose for quick cleanup of stray squirts afterward.

Pasta Collage

AGES: 2–5

DEVELOPMENTAL GOALS:

✄ To promote creativity

✄ To improve gluing techniques

LEARNING OBJECTIVE:

Using pasta, glue, brushes, and heavy paper, the child will create a collage.

MATERIALS:

Pasta of various types
Resealable bags
Bowls
Food coloring or liquid watercolor
Rubbing alcohol
Newspaper
Glue
Brushes
Heavy paper

ADULT PREPARATION:

1. Color the uncooked pasta the day before you use it (see "Helpful Hints," page xii). Children enjoy helping with this process.
2. Place stained pasta in bowls. Use one bowl for each color.
3. Pour glue into separate bowl. Place a brush beside it.

PROCEDURES:

The child will complete the following steps:

1. Spread glue on paper with a brush.
2. Glue colored pasta onto the paper.

Note: Do not dilute the glue for this activity.

Pine Cone Roll

ADULT PREPARATION:

1. Pour tempera paint of various fall colors into containers. Mix the paint with dish soap.
2. Lay paper in the box lid.

PROCEDURES:

The child will complete the following steps:
1. Dip the small end of the pine cone in the paint.
2. Place the painted pine cone on the paper.
3. Roll the pine cone around the paper by tilting the box lid.
4. Repeat steps 1–3 using different pine cones in different colors.

VARIATION:

Pine cone may also be used to brush paint across paper.

AGES: 3–5

DEVELOPMENTAL GOALS:
- To appreciate nature
- To coordinate large and small muscles

LEARNING OBJECTIVE:

Using pine cones, tempera paint, brushes, paper, and a large box lid, the child will paint with different materials.

MATERIALS:

Pine cones
Tempera paint
Dish soap
Containers
Paintbrushes
Paper
Large box lid

Pine Needle Painting

AGES: 2–5

DEVELOPMENTAL GOALS:

✂ To delight in movement

✂ To stimulate cognitive growth through the use of new materials

LEARNING OBJECTIVE:

Using pine needles, rubber bands, tempera paint, and paper, the child will paint in a new way.

MATERIALS:

Pine straw needles or tiny branches
Rubber bands
Tempera paint
Dish soap
Small containers
Paper

ADULT PREPARATION:

1. Place tempera paint of various colors into small containers.

2. Mix paint well with dish soap.

3. Gather pine needles into small bundles, securing the bundles with rubber bands.

PROCEDURES:

The child will complete the following steps:

1. Hold a bundle of pine needles by the rubber-banded end.

2. Dip the pine needles into the paint.

3. Using the pine needles as a brush, paint on the paper.

Note: This activity can be done at the easel or art table.

Pizza Cutter Painting

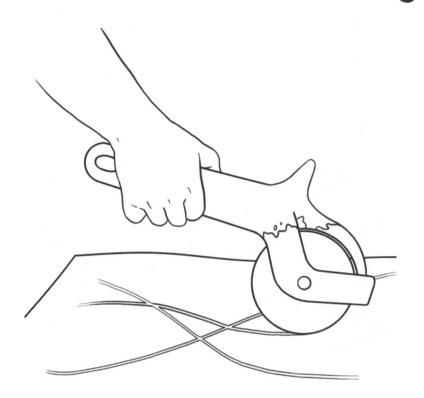

AGES: 3–5

DEVELOPMENTAL GOALS:

✂ To develop the grasping muscles

✂ To use and identify a variety of colors

LEARNING OBJECTIVE:

Using a plastic pizza cutter, tempera paint, and paper, the child will paint with different tools.

MATERIALS:

Plastic pizza cutter
Tempera paint
Dish soap
Foam plates
Paper

ADULT PREPARATION:

1. Pour a small amount of paint on the plate.
2. Mix with dish soap.
3. Prepare several colors of paint, using a separate plate for each color.

PROCEDURES:

The child will complete the following steps:

1. Dip the pizza cutter in the paint.
2. Roll the pizza cutter across the paper.
3. Repeat steps 1–2, using other colors.
4. When asked, identify colors used.

Note: May cut paper in circle to simulate cutting a pizza.

Plastic Pull

DEVELOPMENTAL GOALS:

✄ To experience a new art form

✄ To stimulate the sense of sight

LEARNING OBJECTIVE:

Using pump soap dispensers, tempera paint, plastic wrap, and paper, the child will pump paint onto the paper and then pull paint across the paper.

MATERIALS:

Empty pump soap dispensers
Dish soap
Tempera paint
Plastic wrap
Paper
Masking tape

ADULT PREPARATION:

1. Mix tempera paint with dish soap.
2. Put each color of paint into a different pump soap dispenser.
3. Tape paper to the table.

PROCEDURES:

The child will complete the following steps:

1. Pump paint of different colors onto paper.
2. Cover the painted paper with plastic wrap.
3. Rub one hand across the plastic and watch the paint spread.
4. Slowly pull the plastic off the paper, leaving a trail of paint behind.

Plunger Prints

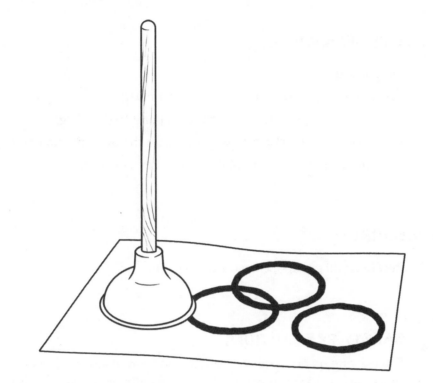

AGES: 2–5

DEVELOPMENTAL GOALS:

✂ To develop creativity

✂ To coordinate large and small muscles

LEARNING OBJECTIVE:

Using plungers, tempera paint, and paper, the child will create plunger prints.

MATERIALS:

New bathroom plungers (only used for painting)
Tempera paint
Dish soap
Foam plates
Paper towels
Paper

ADULT PREPARATION:

1. Make paint blotters in different colors (see "Helpful Hints," page xi).
2. Place plungers on blotters.

PROCEDURES:

The child will complete the following steps:

1. Press the plunger onto the paint blotter.
2. Make a circle on the paper by pressing the plunger on the paper.
3. Repeat with other colors.

Note: You may want to do this activity outside on the ground, or on the floor. The long-handled plungers are difficult for small children to use on the table. If used as an indoor floor activity, lay newspaper or a plastic sheet on the floor before putting down the paper.

Popcorn Mosaic

AGES: 4–5

DEVELOPMENTAL GOALS:

✂ To develop eye-hand coordination

✂ To improve gluing techniques

LEARNING OBJECTIVE:

Using popcorn, glue, and paper, the child will create a mosaic.

MATERIALS:

Dry tempera paint
Resealable plastic bags
Glue
Popcorn
Paper
Spoons
Plates, small trays, or bowls

ADULT PREPARATION:

1. Pop popcorn.
2. Place popped popcorn in resealable plastic bags.
3. Add a heaping spoonful of dry tempera paint to each bag.
4. Shake bag until the popcorn is coated with the dry tempera paint.
5. Pour colored popcorn onto plates, small trays, or bowls.

PROCEDURE:

1. The child will glue popcorn onto the paper.

⚠ SAFETY PRECAUTION:

The use of popcorn requires close supervision. Popcorn has been known to cause choking in young children. If children are permitted to eat popcorn, provide undyed popcorn. Check the school's policies regarding popcorn.

Popcorn Painting

ADULT PREPARATION:

1. Pop popcorn.
2. Place popped popcorn in small bowls.
3. Spread a thin layer of tempera paint in different colors onto plates or small trays.
4. Mix dish soap into the paint.

PROCEDURES:

The child will complete the following steps:

1. Dip a piece of popcorn into paint.
2. Press the popcorn onto paper, making a print.
3. Repeat steps 1–2 with other colors.

 ## SAFETY PRECAUTION:

The use of popcorn requires close supervision. Popcorn has been known to cause choking in young children.

AGES: 3–5

DEVELOPMENTAL GOALS:

- ✄ To develop eye-hand coordination
- ✄ To stimulate small muscle development

LEARNING OBJECTIVE:

Using tempera paint, popcorn, and paper, the child will paint with popcorn.

MATERIALS:

Tempera paint
Dish soap
Foam plates or
small trays
Popcorn
Paper
Small bowls

DEVELOPMENTAL GOALS:

✂ To stimulate the sense of smell

✂ To improve gluing techniques

LEARNING OBJECTIVE:

Using unsweetened powdered drink mix, diluted glue, brushes, a spoon, and paper, the child will paint with liquids other than paint.

MATERIALS:

Unsweetened powdered drink mix in several colors

Small containers

Glue

Water

Wide brushes

Spoons

Paper

Powdered Drink Mix Painting

ADULT PREPARATION:

1. Pour powdered drink mix into small containers.
2. Dilute glue with water (two parts glue to one part water). Pour into small containers (not the ones containing powdered drink mix).

PROCEDURES:

The child will complete the following steps:

1. Brush diluted glue onto paper.
2. Sprinkle powdered drink mix onto paper with spoon.

Notes: Powdered drink mix may be put into empty salt shakers.

Flavored gelatin mixes may be used instead of powdered drink mixes for different scents.

Powdered Drink Mix Play Dough

PROCEDURES:

With an adult's help, the child will complete the following steps:
1. Mix dry ingredients.
2. Add water and vegetable oil.
3. Knead on wax paper to desired consistency.
4. Store at room temperature in sealed containers or resealable plastic bags labeled with each child's name (to prevent the spread of disease).

Note: It is not necessary to use boiling water to make this dough. Hot water from the tap produces the same results and is safer for children to use.

 SAFETY PRECAUTION:
Temperature of tap water varies. Test the dough before children knead it to ensure it is not too hot.

AGES: 3–5 to make the dough; 1–5 to play with the dough

DEVELOPMENTAL GOALS:

- ✂ To develop self-help skills
- ✂ To feel a sense of accomplishment

LEARNING OBJECTIVE:

Using flour, salt, vegetable oil, hot water, unsweetened powdered drink mix, a bowl, measuring cups, measuring spoons, and wax paper, the child will create scented play dough.

MATERIALS:

2½ cups flour
1 cup salt
3 teaspoons vegetable oil
2 cups hot water
2 standard size packages unsweetened powdered drink mix
Bowl
Measuring cups
Measuring spoons
Wax paper

Pudding Puff Painting

AGES: 1–5

DEVELOPMENTAL GOALS:

✂ To stimulate the sense of touch

✂ To experience a new art form

LEARNING OBJECTIVE:

Using pudding mixture, a nylon bath puff, and paper, the child will paint with a new medium.

MATERIALS:

Instant pudding mix
Milk
Measuring cups
Spoons
Bowl
Paper plate
Nylon bath puff
Paper

ADULT PREPARATION:

1. Mix pudding with milk, in the bowl, according to package directions.
2. Refrigerate until needed.
3. Put pudding on a paper plate.

PROCEDURES:

The child will complete the following steps:

1. Dip the nylon bath puff into the pudding.
2. Press the puff onto the paper.
3. Repeat steps 1–2.

ACTIVITY SUGGESTION:

Using chocolate pudding creates the look of mud for a farm or gardening unit.

continued

106

Pudding Puff Painting continued

VARIATION:

Use pudding as edible finger paint. Make sure each child has his or her own source of pudding by putting pudding on individual plates. This will help to eliminate the spread of germs.

Quarter Prints

AGES: 3–5

DEVELOPMENTAL GOALS:

✂ To follow directions

✂ To develop eye-hand coordination

LEARNING OBJECTIVE:

Using quarters, tape, newsprint or copy paper, and crayons, the child will create prints.

MATERIALS:

Quarters
Two-sided tape or masking tape
Newsprint or copy paper
Crayons with paper wrappings removed

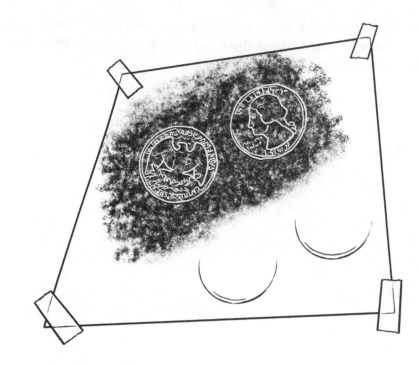

ADULT PREPARATION:

1. Tape quarters to tabletop or tray by placing tape under the quarters (either two-sided tape or a loop of masking tape). Do not tape over the tops of quarters.

2. Place paper over quarters.

3. Secure edges of paper with tape so paper will not move.

PROCEDURE:

The child will complete the following step:

1. Lay crayon on its side and rub lightly over the paper. (If crayon is held straight up, the quarter's design will not show through the rubbing.)

Note: Any type of coin may be used to make this rubbing print.

VARIATION:

Use aluminum foil instead of paper and rub with a cotton swab.

108

Quill Painting

AGES: 2–5

DEVELOPMENTAL GOALS:

✄ To develop prewriting skills

✄ To improve fine motor control

LEARNING OBJECTIVE:

Using large feathers, tempera paint, and paper, the child will paint with a quill.

MATERIALS:

Large feathers with pronounced tips
Tempera paint (several colors)
Dish soap
Small containers
Paper

ADULT PREPARATION:

1. Pour tempera paint into small containers. Mix with soap.
2. Place at least one feather beside each paint container.

PROCEDURES:

The child will complete the following steps:

1. Dip feather's point into paint.
2. Draw with feather's point on paper.
3. Repeat with different quills and paint of other colors.

Note: This activity can be done at the easel or art table.

Quilt Art

DEVELOPMENTAL GOALS:

- ✄ To participate in a group project
- ✄ To develop creativity

LEARNING OBJECTIVE:

Using paper, markers, crayons, tempera paint, and brushes, the children will create a quilt.

MATERIALS:

Paper
Markers
Crayons
Tempera paint or
  watercolors
Dish soap
Brushes and/or cotton
  swabs

ADULT PREPARATION:

1. Mix soap and tempera paint together.
2. Cut paper into equal squares.
3. Give each child his or her own square.

PROCEDURES:

The child will complete the following steps:

1. Use markers, crayons, and/or paints to create a design on his or her square.
2. Working with others or by taking his or her turn, glue the square onto a large sheet of bulletin board paper to make a group design.

VARIATIONS:

Individual quilts may be made by collecting one square from each child each month. These are put together for an end-of-the-year gift. Cloth squares may be made with handprints painted by a child each month and sewn together by the teacher for individual parent's day gifts.

Record Player Art

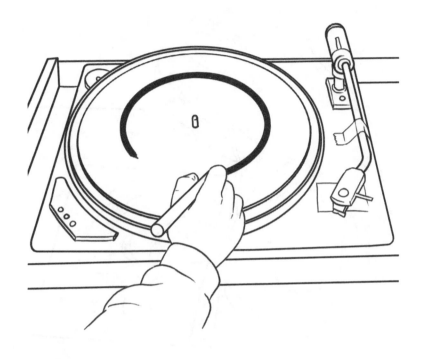

R

AGES: 2–5

DEVELOPMENTAL
GOALS:

✄ To experience a new
   art form

✄ To develop eye-hand
   coordination

LEARNING
OBJECTIVE:

Using record player,
paper plate, masking
tape, crayons, markers,
colored pencils, gel
pens, watercolors, and
brushes, the child will
create a spin art design.

MATERIALS:

Record player
Paper plate or paper cut
   to fit on the
   turntable
Masking tape
Crayons, markers,
   colored pencils,
   gel pens
Food coloring or liquid
   watercolors
Small brushes or cotton
   swabs

ADULT PREPARATION:

1. Tape the arm of the record player to immobilize it.
2. Poke a hole in the center of the paper plate or paper.
3. Fold masking tape and put on the back of the plate or paper.
4. Put plate or paper (tape side down) on turntable.
5. Turn the record player on.

PROCEDURES:

The child will complete the following steps:

1. As the record player rotates the plate, hold the marker (or crayon,
   pen, or pencil) lightly on the plate and watch as a design spins forth.
2. Repeat with other colors.

Roller Painting

AGES: 1–5

DEVELOPMENTAL GOALS:

✄ To develop creativity

✄ To develop fine motor control

LEARNING OBJECTIVE:

Using roll-on deodorant bottles, diluted tempera paint, and paper, the child will roll paint across the paper.

MATERIALS:

Roll-on deodorant bottles
Tempera paint
Water
Paper

ADULT PREPARATION:

1. Pop the roller ball out of each deodorant bottle.
2. Fill with tempera paint diluted with water (two parts paint to one part water).
3. Replace the ball.

PROCEDURES:

The child will complete the following steps:

1. Holding the bottle upside down, roll the paint onto the paper in the desired design.
2. Repeat with other colors.

Note: This activity can be done at the easel or art table.

Rope Painting

ADULT PREPARATION:

1. Put tempera paint into separate containers.
2. Mix with dish soap.
3. Cut rope into different lengths, but each should be less than 12 inches.
4. Pull ends of cut rope to fray.

PROCEDURES:

The child will complete the following steps:
1. Dip frayed rope into tempera paint.
2. Using the rope as a brush, spread paint on paper.
3. Repeat with other colors.

Note: This may be done at the easel or art table.

 SAFETY PRECAUTION:
Using rope lengths less than 12 inches ensures that the child cannot harm himself or herself with the rope.

AGES: 1–5

DEVELOPMENTAL GOALS:

- ✂ To improve small muscle skills
- ✂ To feel competent in motor control

LEARNING OBJECTIVE:

Using frayed rope, tempera paint, and paper, the child will experience a new way to paint.

MATERIALS:

Frayed rope in different sizes and textures
Tempera paint
Dish soap
Paper
Small containers

DEVELOPMENTAL GOALS:

✂ To develop creativity

✂ To develop small muscles

LEARNING OBJECTIVE:

Using rubber bands, wooden blocks, tempera paint, and paper, the child will create prints.

MATERIALS:

Rubber bands of various widths

Wooden block (more blocks can be used to make several different designs)

Tempera paint

Dish soap

Foam plate or tray

Paper towel

Paper

Rubber Band Block Prints

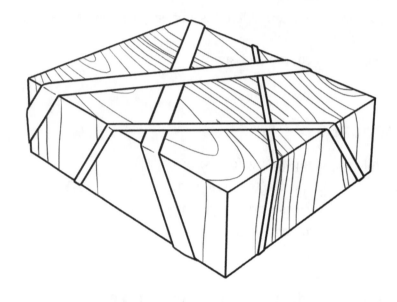

ADULT PREPARATION:

1. Make a paint blotter (see "Helpful Hints," page xi).
2. Place rubber bands around block in desired pattern.

PROCEDURES:

The child will complete the following steps:

1. Place block with rubber band design on paint blotter.
2. Press the block onto paper.
3. Repeat steps 2–3 with different colors.

continued

Rubber Band Block Prints continued

**Notes: Stamp pads may be used instead of the paint blotter.
Older children may place rubber bands on the block.**

ACTIVITY SUGGESTION:

During a transportation unit, the rubber bands may be placed to resemble a railroad track so that a railroad track print can be created.

Salad Spinner Art

AGES: 2–5

DEVELOPMENTAL GOALS:

✄ To experience a new art form

✄ To develop eye-hand coordination

LEARNING OBJECTIVE:

Using a salad spinner, masking tape, paper, tempera paint, and spoons, the child will create spin art.

MATERIALS:

Salad spinner (either battery powered or manual; if manual type is used, be sure it has a large handle, which is easier for a child to turn)
Masking tape
Paper cut to fit inside the salad spinner, or small paper plate
Tempera paint
Spoons or squirt bottles

ADULT PREPARATION:

1. Mix tempera paint with water. Experiment with the consistency. It needs to be thicker than watercolor but somewhat diluted in order to squirt out of the bottle.

2. Tape paper to the bottom of the salad spinner basket.

PROCEDURES:

The child will complete the following steps:

1. Squirt or spoon several *small* amounts of color onto paper (large amounts may become one big blob on the paper).

2. Put the lid on the spinner (with adult assistance, if necessary).

3. Turn on or crank the spinner (with adult assistance, if necessary).

4. Remove lid and look at design.

5. Repeat steps 1–4 with other colors, if desired.

Salt Art

ADULT PREPARATION:

1. Pour salt into resealable bags or containers. Fill each three-fourths full, leaving room to add dry tempera paint.
2. Add dry tempera paint. Shake or stir until salt and dry paint are mixed together.
3. Pour colored salt into bowls.

PROCEDURES:

The child will complete the following steps:

1. Spoon different colors of the salt and paint mixture into a baby food jar, in layers, leaving a space of ¼ inch at the top of the jar.
2. Fill the ¼" space at the top of the jar with glue (with adult assistance, if necessary), to prevent the salt from shifting.
3. Allow glue to dry.
4. Put lid on baby food jar.

VARIATIONS:

The salt and paint mixture may be glued on heavy paper like a mosaic.
The salt and paint mixture can be put into a shaker (one shaker per color) and then sprinkled on the paper.
White sand may be used in place of salt.

AGES: 3–5

DEVELOPMENTAL GOALS:
- ✄ To enhance fine muscle skills
- ✄ To improve gluing techniques

LEARNING OBJECTIVE:

Using salt, dry tempera paint, glue, spoons, and small clear jars with lids, the child will experience a new art form.

MATERIALS:
Table salt
Dry tempera paint
Baby food jars with lids or small clear plastic jars with lids
Resealable plastic bags or containers with lids
Bowls
Spoons
White school glue

Shaving Cream Tie-Dye

DEVELOPMENTAL GOALS:

✂ To increase creativity

✂ To stimulate muscle development

LEARNING OBJECTIVE:

Using shaving cream, liquid watercolors, squirt bottles, scraper, and paper, the child will experience a new art form.

MATERIALS:

Shaving cream (nonmenthol)
Foam plate or small tray
Liquid watercolors in small squirt bottles
Scraper (a ruler or spatula can be used)
Paper

ADULT PREPARATION:

1. Shake can of shaving cream.
2. Squirt shaving cream onto plate.
3. Drizzle liquid watercolors onto shaving cream. Do not mix the colors into the shaving cream.

PROCEDURES:

The child will complete the following steps:

1. Press the paper onto shaving cream.
2. Scrape excess shaving cream off paper (a younger child may need adult assistance).

continued

Shaving Cream Tie-Dye continued

3. Look at the design created (the color remains on the paper).
4. Repeat steps 1–3 if desired.

Note: The shaving cream and colors need to be wiped off the plate/tray between each child. Shake the can often, so the shaving cream does not become flat.

VARIATION:

Shaving cream can also be used as fingerpaint on a tray or put directly on the tabletop. This cleans off any excess glue or other material from the table. Be sure to have a water source available for easy cleanup.

Soap Art Fingerpainting

DEVELOPMENTAL GOALS:

- ✂ To express emotions through art
- ✂ To relieve tension

LEARNING OBJECTIVE:

Using pump soap dispensers, dish soap, tempera paint, and paper, the child will use new materials to fingerpaint.

MATERIALS:

Empty pump soap dispensers
Dish detergent
White tempera paint
Paper

ADULT PREPARATION:

1. Mix white tempera paint with two tablespoons of liquid dish detergent.
2. Fill the pump soap dispensers with the tempera paint and dish soap mixture.

PROCEDURES:

The child will complete the following steps:

1. Pump the tempera paint and dish soap mixture onto the paper.
2. Spread the mixture with both hands.

Note: Paint will wash off easily with dish soap mixed into it.

120

Sock Painting

AGES: 3–5

DEVELOPMENTAL GOALS:

- ✂ To increase control of the body
- ✂ To enhance large muscle development

LEARNING OBJECTIVE:

Using socks, tempera paint, and paper, the child will walk paint across paper.

MATERIALS:

Old socks (ask parents to provide unmatched socks of different textures)
Tempera paint
Dish soap
Plates or trays
Plastic tarp or shower curtain
Long sheet of paper (newsprint roll, or bulletin board paper)
Chairs
Pan of soapy water
Bath towels

ADULT PREPARATION:

1. Mix tempera paint with dish soap.
2. Put paint mixture in different colors on paper plates, one color per plate.
3. Lay plastic tarp or shower curtain on floor.
4. Put long sheet of paper on top of tarp.
5. Place a chair near each end of the paper.
6. Place paint plates near one chair.
7. Place towels and the pan of soapy water near the other chair.

PROCEDURES:

The child will complete the following steps:

1. Remove shoes and socks.
2. If long pants are worn, roll them up.
3. Put "school socks" on feet.

continued

121

Sock Painting continued

4. Sit in chair near plates of paint.

5. Put each foot into a different plate of paint.

6. Remove feet from plate of paint.

7. Step onto paper and then walk across paper to other chair.

8. With adult assistance, take off and discard painted socks, which may be thrown away or washed and used another time.

9. Place feet in soapy water and wash off any excess paint (with adult assistance, if necessary).

10. Dry feet with towel.

11. Put regular socks and shoes back on.

VARIATION:

This activity can be done outside.

Spin Top Painting

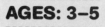

AGES: 3–5

DEVELOPMENTAL GOALS:

✂ To develop creativity

✂ To increase fine motor control

LEARNING OBJECTIVE:

Using spin tops, tempera paint, and paper, the child will paint by spinning tops.

MATERIALS:

Spin tops (one for each tempera paint color)
Tempera paint in several colors
Dish soap
Plates
Paper

ADULT PREPARATION:

1. Pour a small amount of paint onto each plate.
2. Mix paint with dish soap.
3. Set a spin top beside each color of paint.

PROCEDURES:

The child will complete the following steps:

1. Dip spin top in the paint.
2. Spin the top on the paper.
3. Repeat steps 1–2 with different colors.

ACTIVITY SUGGESTION:

Spin the tops with fluorescent or bright colors of tempera paint on black paper to create the illusion of fireworks, for Chinese New Year or Independence Day units.

Spray Painting

Ages: 2–5

DEVELOPMENTAL GOALS:

- ✂ To enhance eye-hand coordination
- ✂ To stimulate the growth of small muscles

LEARNING OBJECTIVE:

Using diluted tempera paint, spray bottles, and paper, the child will spray paint.

MATERIALS:

Tempera paint or liquid watercolor
Water
Spray bottles—one for each color
Paper

ADULT PREPARATION:

1. Dilute tempera paint with water to a watercolor consistency and put into spray bottles (if using liquid watercolor, do not dilute).

PROCEDURES:

The child will complete the following steps:

1. Spray paper with paint.
2. Repeat with other colors.

Note: Select spray bottles that pump easily.

ACTIVITY SUGGESTION:

For a Mother Goose ("Rain, Rain, Go Away") or weather unit, tint the water blue and have the child spray the tinted water onto the paper like raindrops.

VARIATIONS:

This activity can be done outside, with the paper taped to a chain link fence.

This activity may also be done at the easel with an old shower curtain or piece of plastic taped on the wall behind the easel.

Spray painting may also be done by putting the paper in the bottom of a deep box.

Squirt and Squish Painting

ADULT PREPARATION:

1. Dilute paint with water (two parts paint to one part water).
2. Put into squirt bottles.
3. Fold paper in half.

PROCEDURES:

The child will complete the following steps:

1. Unfold paper.
2. Squirt paint in several colors on one side of the folded paper (a younger child may need adult assistance).
3. Fold paper over paint.
4. Rub the top side of the paper, squishing the paint between the folded paper halves.
5. Open the paper to see the new design.

Note: If too much paint is used, it will squish out the sides.

ACTIVITY SUGGESTION:

The symmetrical design of squirt and squish painting resembles a butterfly, so this may be part of a spring unit.

AGES: 2–5

DEVELOPMENTAL GOALS:

- ✄ To follow directions
- ✄ To develop eye-hand coordination

LEARNING OBJECTIVE:

Using squirt bottles, diluted tempera paint, and paper, the child will create a squirt and squish painting.

MATERIALS:

Squirt bottles (can use condiment containers or recycle squeeze bottles such as small shampoo bottles)
Tempera paint
Water
Paper

S

Straw Painting

AGES: 3–5

DEVELOPMENTAL GOALS:

- To perfect the use of a straw
- To practice a new art form

LEARNING OBJECTIVE:

Using a straw, diluted tempera paint, squirt bottles, and paper, the child will blow paint around the paper.

MATERIALS:

Plastic straw
Tempera paint
Water
Squirt bottles or containers with spoons
Paper
Push pin

ADULT PREPARATION:

1. Dilute paint with water and put into squirt bottles or small containers.
2. Check to make sure the child knows how to blow through the straw.
3. Poke a hole near the top of the straw to prevent paint from being drawn up the straw.

PROCEDURES:

The child will complete the following steps:

1. Squirt or spoon a small amount of paint onto the paper.
2. Aim the straw at the paint, and blow the paint around the paper.
3. Repeat using different colors.

continued

Straw Painting continued

Notes: For sanitary purposes, each child should have his or her own straw.

Younger children may get tired of blowing and use the straw as a brush.

Experiment with the consistency of the paint. Some tempera paints are thicker than others. The consistency needs to be thin enough that the child is able to easily blow it around the paper; you don't want it so thin that the paint sprays when blown, however.

ACTIVITY SUGGESTION:

This may be used during a weather unit to discuss wind.

Tin Can Painting

AGES: 2–5

DEVELOPMENTAL GOALS:

✂ To promote creativity

✂ To coordinate large and small muscles

LEARNING OBJECTIVE:

Using tin cans, brushes, tempera paint, and paper, the child will spread paint on the paper.

MATERIALS:

Empty tin cans (not aluminum; must have ridges around them)
Masking tape
Brushes
Tempera paint
Dish soap
Paper
Containers

ADULT PREPARATION:

1. Tape masking tape around sharp edges of empty tin can.
2. Put tempera paint into containers.
3. Mix tempera paint with dish soap.

PROCEDURES:

The child will complete the following steps:

1. Paint can with a brush.
2. Roll can across paper, or wrap thin paper around the can and then press the paper to make a print (with adult assistance, if necessary).
3. Repeat with other colors.

Tissue Paper Art

AGES: 2-5

ADULT PREPARATION:

1. Cut tissue paper of various colors into small pieces.
2. Pour liquid starch or diluted glue into bowls (two parts glue to one part water).

PROCEDURES:

The child will complete the following steps:

1. Brush liquid starch or diluted glue onto paper.
2. Place pieces of tissue paper on top in desired design.

VARIATION:

Lay cut pieces of colored tissue paper on plain white paper, and then spray the pieces of colored tissue paper with water. Let dry, then remove the tissue paper pieces. Their colors will have faded onto the paper. (Do not use fade-resistant tissue paper.)

DEVELOPMENTAL GOALS:

✂ To develop eye-hand coordination

✂ To increase fine motor control

LEARNING OBJECTIVE:

Using tissue paper, liquid starch or diluted glue, a brush, and paper, the child will create tissue paper art.

MATERIALS:

Tissue paper
Liquid starch or diluted glue
Paper
Wide brush
Bowls

T

Toast Painting (Edible Art)

AGES: 2–5

DEVELOPMENTAL GOALS:

- To develop creativity
- To practice cooking procedures

LEARNING OBJECTIVE:

Using bread, milk, food coloring, cotton swabs, cookie sheet, and plate, the child will create edible art.

MATERIALS:

White bread
Whole milk
Food coloring (do not use liquid watercolor)
Cotton swabs
Cookie sheet
Aluminum foil
Plates

ADULT PREPARATION:

1. Mix milk with food coloring. Less food coloring will make a lighter color; more food coloring will make a darker color.
2. Cover cookie sheet with foil.
3. Preheat oven to broil.

PROCEDURES:

The child will complete the following steps:

1. Put bread on plate.
2. Using cotton swabs, decorate bread with milk of different colors.
3. Place bread on cookie sheet.
4. Watch as adult puts cookie sheet under broiler and broils until the bread is toasted.

continued

Toast Painting (Edible Art) continued

Note: When working with a group of children, line cookie sheet with foil and write each child's name on the foil with permanent marker. Place each child's decorated bread above his or her name on the cookie sheet, then broil.

"Toothpaste" Painting

AGES: 1–5

DEVELOPMENTAL GOALS:

✄ To promote self-help skills

✄ To develop small muscle coordination

LEARNING OBJECTIVE:

Using light (colorless) corn syrup, tempera paint, liquid dish soap, toothbrush, and paper, the child will experience the use of new materials to paint.

MATERIALS:

Light corn syrup
White tempera paint
Liquid dish soap
Container
Sandwich bag
Spoon
Toothbrush

ADULT PREPARATION:

1. Put a sandwich bag in container. This is a must for easy cleanup, because corn syrup dries very hard.
2. Mix three parts corn syrup, one part white tempera paint, and one part liquid dish soap in the sandwich bag, with a spoon.
3. Place paper on table or easel.

PROCEDURES:

The child will complete the following steps:

1. Dip toothbrush into mixture.
2. Brush paper with the "toothpaste" mixture.

Note: If the weather is damp, this project may take a few days to dry. When dry, the corn syrup mixture will be glossy, like enamel.

GLUE

Torn Paper Art

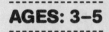

AGES: 3–5

DEVELOPMENTAL GOALS:

✂ To stimulate small muscle development

✂ To improve gluing techniques

LEARNING OBJECTIVE:

Using construction paper, scrap paper, and glue, the child will experience a new art form.

MATERIALS:

Construction paper
Colorful scrap paper (such as old wrapping paper and magazine pages)
Glue
Bowl
Water
Brush

ADULT PREPARATION:

1. Place construction paper, glue, and scrap paper on the table.

PROCEDURES:

The child will complete the following steps:

1. Tear scrap paper into smaller pieces.
2. Glue small pieces onto construction paper.

   (Older children may glue these into a pattern.)

Note: Glue may be diluted (two parts glue to one part water). Then the child may brush glue onto the paper before beginning to tear scrap paper into small pieces.

ACTIVITY SUGGESTIONS:

Set out scrap paper in fall colors for the children to tear and use to create a fall scene. Using pastels may produce a spring scene.

133

T

Track Painting

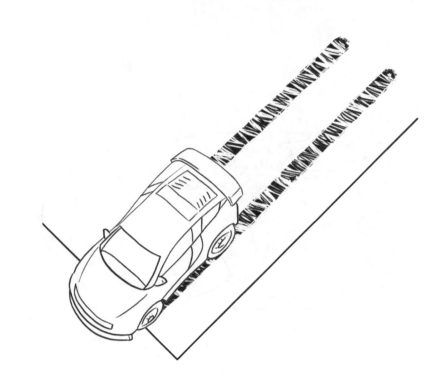

AGES: 1–5

DEVELOPMENTAL GOALS:

- ✂ To delight in movement
- ✂ To coordinate muscle use

LEARNING OBJECTIVE:

Using toy cars, tempera paint, and paper, the child will paint using familiar objects in a new way.

MATERIALS:

Toy cars with movable wheels and different tire treads
Tempera paint
Dish soap
Foam trays or plates
Paper towels
Paper or roll of paper
Drop cloth

ADULT PREPARATION:

1. Make paint blotters in different colors (see "Helpful Hints," page xi).
2. Place drop cloth on floor.
3. Put paper on drop cloth.

PROCEDURES:

The child will complete the following steps:

1. Roll toy car or truck across paint blotter.
2. Roll toy vehicle across paper.
3. Repeat steps 1–2 with other colors.

Note: Using black paper and white or yellow paint can be used to produce paintings resembling blacktopped roads, but any color combination for paper and paint can be used. This activity may be done on a table.

134

Udder Art

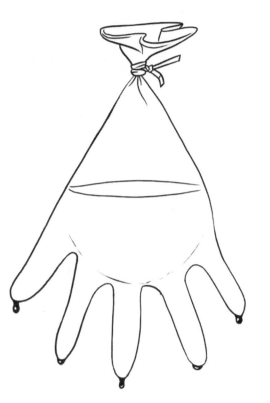

DEVELOPMENTAL GOALS:

- ✂ To interact with an adult
- ✂ To develop and coordinate small muscles

LEARNING OBJECTIVE:

Using a disposable latex or plastic glove, diluted tempera paint, paper, and a box, the child will paint as though milking a cow.

MATERIALS:

Disposable latex or plastic glove
Pushpin
Twist tie
White tempera paint
Water
Dark paper
Box (large enough for 8 X 11 paper)

ADULT PREPARATION:

1. Use pushpin to poke one hole in each fingertip of gloves.
2. Mix two parts white tempera paint with one part water. (If the paint is too thick to go through the holes in the glove, use more water.)
3. Pour diluted white tempera paint into glove, leaving room to seal the top of the glove with a twist tie.
4. Tie top of glove shut with a twist tie.
5. Put dark paper into box.

PROCEDURE:

The child will complete the following step:

1. While adult holds glove slightly above the box, pull on glove fingers, "milking" the paint onto paper.

continued

Udder Art continued

ACTIVITY SUGGESTION:

You may also make and laminate a cutout of a cow. Make a slit where the udder would hang, and then slip the opening of the glove through the slit. Hold onto the opening of the glove, as the child "milks" the cow. This activity may be done on a tarp-covered floor or outdoors instead of in a box.

136

Under the Table Drawing

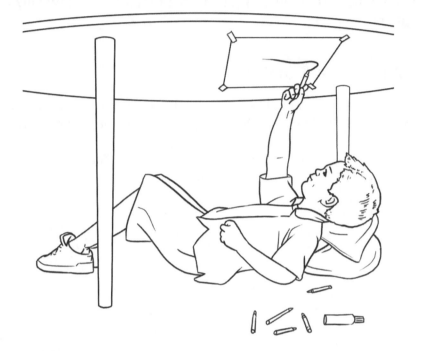

AGES: 2–5

DEVELOPMENTAL GOALS:

✂ To develop social skills

✂ To share physical space with another child

LEARNING OBJECTIVE:

Using pillow, tape, paper, table, crayons, markers, and colored pencils, the child will draw in a new position.

MATERIALS:

Pillow
Masking tape
Paper
Table
Crayons, markers, or colored pencils

ADULT PREPARATION:

1. Tape paper to the underside of the tabletop.
2. Place pillow on floor, under table.
3. Place crayons, markers, or colored pencils near pillow.

PROCEDURE:

The child will complete the following step:

1. Lie on floor underneath table, with head on pillow, and draw on paper taped to underside of tabletop.

continued

137

Under the Table Drawing continued

Notes: Even the most active child will enjoy this activity.

The entire underside of the tabletop may be covered with paper, or one piece of paper may be used per child, depending on the age and ability of the child or group. Younger children require more paper coverage; older children may just need a reminder to draw only on the paper.

ACTIVITY SUGGESTION:

During an Australian unit, show the children where Australia is located on the globe, and tell them it is sometimes called the "Land Down Under."

Vase Design

DEVELOPMENTAL GOALS:

- ✂ To improve gluing techniques
- ✂ To improve fine motor control

LEARNING OBJECTIVE:

Using baby food jar, tissue paper, diluted glue, and brush, the child will create a design on a vase.

MATERIALS:

Baby food jar
Tissue paper in several colors
Glue
Water
Small container
Wide brush
Scissors

ADULT PREPARATION:

1. Pour glue into small container.
2. Dilute two parts glue with one part water. Mix well.
3. Cut colored tissue paper into small pieces.

PROCEDURES:

The child will complete the following steps:

1. Brush glue over entire exterior of baby food jar.
2. Place tissue paper pieces on jar to form desired design.
3. Allow jar to dry, then brush with diluted glue to seal surface.

Note: Any size jar may be used, but younger children need smaller jars to accommodate their shorter attention spans.

Vegetable Prints

AGES: 1–5

DEVELOPMENTAL GOALS:

✂ To increase creativity

✂ To select own materials for creative use

LEARNING OBJECTIVE:

Using tempera paint, vegetables, and paper, the child will create vegetable prints.

MATERIALS:

Tempera paint (for paint blotters), or liquid watercolor or food coloring (for stamp pads)
Dish soap
Paper towels (for paint blotters) or foam shoe inserts (for stamp pads)
Paper
Foam tray or plate
Various vegetables (e.g., bell peppers, broccoli, celery, carrots, cauliflower, ears of corn, mushrooms, onions, radishes)

ADULT PREPARATION:

1. Cut vegetables into pieces 30 minutes before using.
2. Make paint blotters or stamp pads in different colors (see "Helpful Hints," page xi).

PROCEDURES:

The child will complete the following steps:

1. Select a vegetable piece and press it onto paint blotter or stamp pad.
2. Press vegetable piece onto paper.
3. Repeat with other vegetable pieces and other colors.

Note: When stamping with food products, use a foot insert that can either be washed or thrown away. Do not use a commercial stamp pad with food products. A fork or corn holders may be used in the vegetables to employ as handles. Secure the tines of the fork and corn holder securely into the food as a safety precaution.

ACTIVITY SUGGESTIONS:

Cut a bell pepper in half horizontally. Press in a circle pattern.
Add a bow for a wreath.
Use a potato for a St. Patrick's unit.

Wallpaper Art

DEVELOPMENTAL GOALS:

✂ To develop eye-hand coordination

✂ To enact adult roles

LEARNING OBJECTIVE:

Using prepasted wallpaper, water, paper, or a large box, the child will experience a new art form.

MATERIALS:

Prepasted wallpaper
Bowl of water
Large towel
Paper or large box
Scissors

ADULT PREPARATION:

1. Cut wallpaper into desired shapes or size.
2. Lay towel on table. Place wallpaper pieces and the bowl of water on the towel.

PROCEDURES:

The child will complete the following steps:

1. Dip wallpaper piece into water.
2. Press wallpaper piece onto paper or surface of large box.
3. Repeat until paper or box is covered.

Note: If prepasted wallpaper is not available, the child may brush diluted glue on the wallpaper piece before placing it on the box or paper.

Warming Tray Art

DEVELOPMENTAL GOALS:

- ✂ To follow directions
- ✂ To develop small muscle coordination

LEARNING OBJECTIVE:

Using a warming tray, crayons, towels, paper, aluminum foil, and a child-size oven mitt, the child will observe and draw with melting crayons.

MATERIALS:

Warming tray (found in housewares department, thrift store, or garage sale)
Crayons
Three towels
Paper or aluminum foil or wax paper
Child-size oven mitt

ADULT PREPARATION:

1. Remove paper from crayons.
2. Lay towel on table.
3. Place warming tray on towel (to prevent the tray from sliding).
4. Plug in warming tray.
4. Place a folded towel on each side of warming tray, so child can rest an arm on it without getting burned.
5. Place paper in center of warming tray.

PROCEDURES:

The child will complete the following steps:

1. Draw slowly on paper, observing the crayons melting as they are moved across the paper.

Note: If you do not have a warming tray, an electric skillet may be substituted.

continued

Warming Tray Art continued

⊘ SAFETY PRECAUTION:

This activity requires one-to-one supervision. The warming tray should be located in a safe spot where constant supervision is possible. Before beginning this activity, tell the child that the warming tray is hot. Be sure the child is wearing a child-size oven mitt before picking up a crayon. Tape the warming tray's cord to the table with masking or duct tape so the tray will not be accidentally pulled off the table.

VARIATION:

The adult may place an aluminum muffin pan on the warming tray and place broken crayons, separated by color, into each muffin cup. After the crayons melt, the child may dip a cotton swab into the melted crayon mixture and draw on paper with the cotton swab.

Washcloth Painting

DEVELOPMENTAL GOALS:

- ✂ To improve self-help skills
- ✂ To increase eye-hand coordination

LEARNING OBJECTIVE:

Using a washcloth, tempera paint, soap dish, and paper, the child will use a washcloth to paint.

MATERIALS:

Washcloth
White tempera paint
Dish soap
Soap dish
Paper
Scissors

ADULT PREPARATION:

1. Cut washcloth into four pieces.
2. Fold each cloth piece at least once.
3. Mix one to two tablespoons of dish soap with white tempera paint.
4. Place mixture in soap dish.

PROCEDURES:

The child will complete the following steps:

1. Dip washcloth piece into paint mixture.
2. Blot or rub paint onto paper with washcloth piece.

Wax Candle Art

ADULT PREPARATION:

1. Put blue tempera paint into a container.
2. Mix the blue tempera paint with water to a watercolor consistency, stirring with a spoon.

PROCEDURES:

The child will complete the following steps:

1. Draw on white paper with white wax candles.
2. Using a brush, cover the paper with diluted tempera paint to reveal the drawing.

Note: This "magic drawing" amazes children.

AGES: 1–5

DEVELOPMENTAL GOALS:

✀ To increase creativity
✀ To coordinate muscle development

LEARNING OBJECTIVE:

Using wax candles, diluted tempera paint, a brush, and paper, the child will experience a new art form.

MATERIALS:

White wax candles in various sizes
White paper
Blue tempera paint
Water
Container
Brush
Spoon

Wax Paper Art

DEVELOPMENTAL GOALS:

✂ To observe objects repelling water

✂ To encourage fine motor control

LEARNING OBJECTIVE:

Using wax paper, water-based markers, tape, and paper, the child will use common materials in a new way.

MATERIALS:

Wax paper (at least one piece for each child)
Water-based markers
Paper (light colors)
Masking tape

ADULT PREPARATION:

1. Tape wax paper to the table.

PROCEDURES:

The child will complete the following steps:

1. Draw with water-based markers on wax paper.
2. Lay paper on top of wax paper drawing (with adult assistance, if necessary).
3. Carefully press the paper onto the wax paper drawing.
4. Lift paper to see the transfer of color.

Notes: Use smaller pieces of wax paper for younger children to accommodate their shorter attention spans. Throw the wax paper away after each use.

Wet Chalk Drawing

ADULT PREPARATION:

1. Mix boiling water and sugar, two tablespoons sugar to one-half cup water.
2. Stir until sugar is dissolved.
3. Allow mixture to cool.
4. Pour mixture into small bowls.

PROCEDURES:

The child will complete the following steps:
1. Dip one end of chalk into the mixture.
2. Draw on paper with moistened end of chalk.
3. Repeat steps 1–2 until design is complete, using different colors.

Notes: Mixture may be made the day before. Do not refrigerate; keep at room temperature.

Using the mixture creates brighter, more vivid colors than just using plain water.

AGES: 1–5

DEVELOPMENTAL GOALS:
- ✂ To improve eye-hand coordination
- ✂ To encourage small muscle development

LEARNING OBJECTIVE:
Using sugar solution, chalk, and paper, the child will draw with wet chalk.

MATERIALS:
Boiling water
Sugar
Small bowls
Colored chalk
Paper

Whipped Cream Painting

AGES: 1–5

DEVELOPMENTAL GOALS:

✂ To improve fine motor skills

✂ To enhance creativity

LEARNING OBJECTIVE:

Using whipped topping, liquid coloring, brushes, and paper, the child will paint using a new medium.

MATERIALS:

Whipped topping
Small containers
Liquid watercolor or
    food coloring
Spoon
Brushes
Paper

ADULT PREPARATION:

1. Divide whipped topping into small containers.
2. Using a spoon, add liquid watercolor or food coloring to each container of whipped topping, mixing well.

PROCEDURES:

The child will complete the following steps:

1. Dip brush into colored whipped topping.
2. Apply whipped topping to paper.

Notes: This may also be an individual fingerpainting activity.

Shaving cream may be substituted for whipped topping.

148

Worm Prints

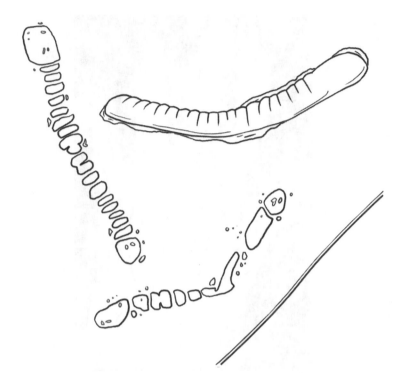

AGES: 2–5

DEVELOPMENTAL GOALS:

✂ To increase creativity

✂ To develop eye-hand coordination

LEARNING OBJECTIVE:

Using plastic worms, stamp pad, and paper, the child will create worm prints.

MATERIALS:

Plastic worms
Liquid watercolor
Foam shoe insert
Foam plate
Paper

ADULT PREPARATION:

1. Make a stamp pad (see "Helpful Hints," page xi).

PROCEDURES:

The child will complete the following steps:

1. Press worm on stamp pad.
2. Press worm on paper, leaving print.
3. Repeat steps 1–2 to add other prints.

X-Ray Drawing

AGES: 1–5

DEVELOPMENTAL GOALS:

- ✀ To strengthen small muscles
- ✀ To improve eye-hand coordination

LEARNING OBJECTIVE:

Using an X-ray and dry erase markers, the child will experience a new art form.

MATERIALS:

Old X-rays (obtained from doctor or dentist)
Dry erase markers
Damp cloth

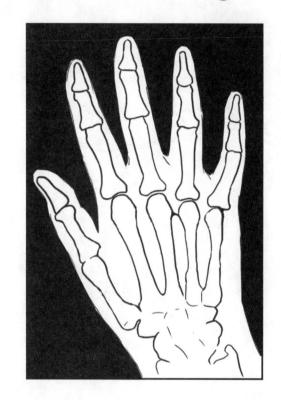

ADULT PREPARATION:

1. Roll child's sleeves up before beginning the activity, to prevent paint from coming off on sleeves if arms are dragged across the marked film during drawing.

PROCEDURES:

1. Child uses dry erase markers to draw on X-ray.
2. May be erased with damp cloth for next child to use.

VARIATIONS:

Mix two parts liquid dish soap and one part white tempera paint. Paint hand with mixture and press onto black paper to make an "X-ray." Using more soap than paint makes the print look translucent.

Xylophone Painting

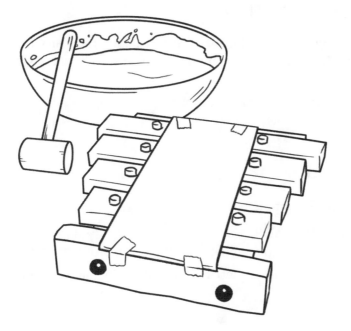

AGES: 3–5

DEVELOPMENTAL GOALS:

✂ To delight in rhythm and music

✂ To create art in various forms

LEARNING OBJECTIVE:

Using toy xylophone and mallet, tempera paint, and paper, the child will create musical tones while painting.

MATERIALS:

Toy xylophone and mallet
Tempera paint
Dish soap
Small containers
Masking tape
Paper

ADULT PREPARATION:

1. Put tempera paint, mixed with dish soap, into small containers.
2. Tape one piece of paper across the keys of the xylophone.

PROCEDURES:

The child will complete the following steps:

1. Dip xylophone mallet into paint.
2. Hit paper-covered xylophone with painted mallet.
3. Move mallet around the xylophone to make additional paint marks, thus hearing different tones.

Yarn Mosaic

AGES: 1–5

DEVELOPMENTAL GOALS:

✂ To improve fine muscle skills

✂ To improve gluing techniques

LEARNING OBJECTIVE:

Using yarn, glue, and tag board, the child will create a mosaic.

MATERIALS:

Yarn of various colors and textures
Scissors
Glue
Small container or bowl
Tag board, cardboard, or very sturdy paper

ADULT PREPARATION:

1. Cut tag board, cardboard, or sturdy paper into a size that matches the child's attention span: the younger the child, the shorter the attention span.
2. Cut yarn into different lengths.

PROCEDURES:

The child will complete the following steps:

1. Dip yarn into glue.
2. Press yarn onto tag board, cardboard, or sturdy paper.
3. Repeat with other pieces of yarn to fill the paper, creating a yarn mosaic.

⚠ SAFETY PRECAUTION:

Do not cut yarn into lengths greater than 12 inches to prevent choking hazards.

Yo-Yo Art

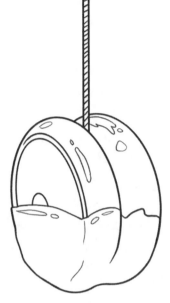

AGES: 3–5

DEVELOPMENTAL GOALS:

✂ To develop rhythm in movement

✂ To control and coordinate muscles

LEARNING OBJECTIVE:

Using a yo-yo, tempera paint, and paper, the child will paint with a new tool.

MATERIALS:

Yo-yo
Tempera paint
Dish soap
Foam trays or plates
Drop cloth
Paper

ADULT PREPARATION:

1. Pour paint into foam trays. Mix with dish soap.
2. Put drop cloth on floor.
3. Put paper on drop cloth.

PROCEDURES:

The child will complete the following steps:

1. Dip yo-yo into paint.
2. Swing yo-yo across paper like a pendulum.
3. Repeat steps 1–2.

Note: This activity may be done outside or by placing the paper in a large box with high sides to help contain the swinging action.

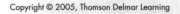

Yogurt Fingerpainting

AGES: 2–5

DEVELOPMENTAL GOALS:

✂ To express emotions through art

✂ To relieve stress and tension

LEARNING OBJECTIVE:

Using yogurt and paper, the child will enjoy a sensory experience while painting.

MATERIALS:

Flavored yogurt (dark-colored flavors work best)
White paper
Tray or plate
Spoon

ADULT PREPARATION:

1. Spoon yogurt onto tray or plate.

PROCEDURES:

The child will complete the following steps:

1. Fingerpaint with yogurt on the tray or plate.
2. Lay paper on top of the fingerpainted design.
3. Press paper onto yogurt.
4. Remove paper and look at design.

VARIATIONS:

The child may fingerpaint directly onto the paper.

⚠ SAFETY PRECAUTION:

Child may try to eat the yogurt. If the yogurt has been placed on a clean individual plate, it should not cause the child any harm.

Zebra Crayon Resist

AGES: 1–5

DEVELOPMENTAL GOALS:

✂ To build creativity

✂ To increase muscle strength

LEARNING OBJECTIVE:

Using paper, wax candle, and diluted tempera paint, the child will experience a new art form.

MATERIALS:

White paper
White wax candle or white crayon
Black tempera paint
Water

ADULT PREPARATION:

1. Dilute black tempera paint with water to watercolor consistency.

PROCEDURES:

The child will complete the following steps:

1. Draw stripes on white paper with white wax candle or white crayon.
2. Paint over stripes with diluted black paint. Wax stripes will resist the paint and remain white.

Notes: May be used as a math activity by drawing a specific number of stripes or creating a pattern by varying the thickness of stripes. Because this is a two-step activity, younger children require smaller pieces of paper to accommodate their shorter attention spans.

VARIATION:

For a pond or ocean unit, vary the medium by using green crayons and blue tempera paint.

Zigzag Art

AGES: 1–5

DEVELOPMENTAL GOALS:

✄ To promote muscle development

✄ To practice various art forms

LEARNING OBJECTIVE:

Using a cardboard tube, rick rack, tempera paint, and paper, the child will create zigzag lines.

MATERIALS:

Toilet tissue tube or similar size tube
Glue
Rickrack (found in fabric stores)
Tempera paint
Dish soap
Foam tray or plate
Paper towel
Paper

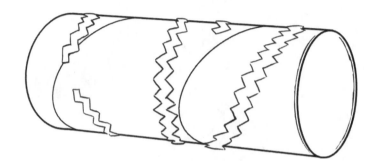

ADULT PREPARATION:

1. Glue rick rack around several cardboard toilet tissue tubes. The strip should be glued all around the tubes in several rows. Let dry.

2. Make a paint blotter (see "Helpful Hints," page xi).

PROCEDURES:

The child will complete the following steps:

1. Roll cardboard toilet tissue tube on paint blotter.

2. Roll cardboard tube on paper, creating a zigzag pattern.

Note: Make several rick rack tubes, and when the cardboard roll gets too wet, you can replace it.

Theme-Specific Index

Index